In the Ima

and the

Shadow of Demons

A Metaphysical Study
of
Good and Evil

Kathy L. Callahan, Ph.D.

Spirit Song Publications
Co-published with Trafford Publishing

Edgar Cayce Readings, Copyrighted © Edgar Cayce Foundation, 1971, 1993, 1994, 1995, 1996.
Used by permission. Edgar Cayce Reading numbers are indicated in the text or follow the quotation in parentheses, i.e. (123-4). The first series of digits indicates the person for whom the reading was given or the series number of the reading. The second digit indicates the sequential reading number.

Unless otherwise indicated, all Scripture quotations are from *The Holy Bible, Revised Standard Version,* copyright © 1952 by the Division of Christian Education of the National Council of the Churches of Christ in the United States of America. Quotations marked KJV are from *The King James Version of the Bible,* copyright © 1958, The National Publishing Company.

Note for Librarians: a cataloguing record for this book that includes Dewey Classification and US Library of Congress numbers is available from the National Library of Canada. The complete cataloguing record can be obtained from the National Library's online database at: www.nlc-bnc.ca/amicus/index-e.html

ISBN 1-4120-1751-3

TRAFFORD

This book was published *on-demand* in cooperation with Trafford Publishing. On-demand publishing is a unique process and service of making a book available for retail sale to the public taking advantage of on-demand manufacturing and Internet marketing. **On-demand publishing** includes promotions, retail sales, manufacturing, order fulfilment, accounting and collecting royalties on behalf of the author.

Suite 6E, 2333 Government St., Victoria, B.C. V8T 4P4, CANADA
Phone   250-383-6864   Toll-free   1-888-232-4444 (Canada & US)
Fax   250-383-6804   E-mail   sales@trafford.com
Web site   www.trafford.com   TRAFFORD PUBLISHING IS A DIVISION OF TRAFFORD HOLDINGS LTD.
Trafford Catalogue #03-2128   www.trafford.com/robots/03-2128.html

10   9   8   7   6   5   4

For we are not contending against flesh and blood, but against the principalities, against the powers, against the world rulers of this present darkness, against the spiritual hosts of wickedness in the heavenly places.
Ephesians 6:12

This book is dedicated to the victims
of the September 11, 2001
terrorist attacks on
the World Trade Center,
the Pentagon,
and United Airlines Flight 93,
their loved ones and
the friends left behind,
the New York City Police Department,
the New York City Fire Department,
the American Red Cross,
and the many other workers
involved in rescue and relief efforts.

Also by Kathy L. Callahan, Ph.D.

Living in the Spirit,
Applying Spiritual Truth in Daily Life
Spirit Song Publications
In conjunction with Trafford Publishing, 2002

Our Origin and Destiny:
An Evolutionary Perspective on the New Millennium
A.R.E. Press, 1996

Unseen Hands and Unknown Hearts,
A Miracle of Healing Created through Prayer
A.R.E. Press, 1995

A.R.E. website:

http://www.edgarcayce.org

or call

A.R.E. Press
1-800-723-1112

ACKNOWLEDGEMENTS

There are many people who have made contributions to this book since its inception five years ago. I would like to thank Twila Holbrook, Woody Oakes, Lynne Plante, Tino Aragon, and Deirdre Aragon for being a sounding board for the ideas contained herein. A thank you also goes out to the many people who have attended my lectures and workshops, as the discussions they generate always contribute to my writing.

A special thank you to my editor, Darcie L. Callahan, not only for her editing skills but also for the many literary recommendations she made which improved the clarity of expression of ideas and enhanced the quality of writing.

Thank you to the Edgar Cayce Foundation for granting extensive copyright permission for excerpts from the Edgar Cayce Readings.

CONTENTS

Author's Foreword

*Spiritual advancement is not restricted
to increasing light in the world;
We need also to increase awareness of those
shadow forces with whom we must wrestle.*
Matthew Fox, <u>Sins of the Spirit; Blessings of the Flesh</u>

Until recently, many Americans gave little thought to questions of good and evil. Such philosophical issues simply did not play a significant role in our daily thoughts. There may have been a particular headline or a certain news story that caused us to wonder, just for a moment, about the evil we see in this world. We live in a secular world, however, and our concerns are mundane ones. The challenges of daily life are simply too overwhelming to allow us much time to reflect on philosophical issues. The events of September 11, 2001, however, changed that.

The unexpectedness and ferocity of the terrorist attacks against the United States changed the way Americans look at life. The tragic loss of innocent life, the heroic efforts of valiant rescue workers, the sacrifice of those brave passengers on United Airlines Flight 93, and the pain felt by loved ones left behind became foremost in our minds. Americans from all walks of life, regardless of race, religion, or ethnic background, put aside petty differences and united as one people. We cried together and prayed together, holding on to one another in our shock and grief.

In the days that followed, we began to question how this had come to pass, and perhaps more importantly, "why." With growing fear, we realized that these actions might very well be the first step in a war of terrorism unleashed against us. Americans suddenly became aware that the political acts of violence common in other countries could occur within our own borders. Our once safe world was gone. In its place was a world of uncertainty and mistrust.

In the months that followed, Americans sought to return to a life of normalcy. There were new security measures to contend with and a sudden increase in disaster drills run by hospitals, fire departments, and other government agencies. People became more observant and aware of their surroundings. For the most part, however, we returned to our familiar routines and our daily activities remain much the same as they were before that tragic day. Yet the events of September 11th were to have a lingering effect upon the way many Americans think. In the blink of an eye, the world, and our perspective of it, had changed. We would never again view life in quite the same way.

Face to Face with Evil

I believe that one of the most significant aspects of the September 11th terrorist attacks is that it brought Americans face to face with evil, perhaps for the first time in our lives. I don't mean to imply we weren't aware of evil prior to this. Our recent experiences with evil, however, have been with what I call "remote evil" and "insane evil." Remote evil includes ancient and modern historic events such as the persecution of innocents for religious reasons, the injustices of slavery, and the carnage that accompanies any war. Recent events include the Holocaust, Stalin's purges, the Cambodian killing fields, the aftermath of China's Cultural Revolution, and recent ethnic cleansing campaigns in Eastern Europe and Africa. Insane evil encompasses those more limited actions committed against individuals, such as murder, rape, and theft.

The events of September 11th, however, brought us face to face with another kind of evil—personal evil. As President George W. Bush said in a speech given that fateful day, "...our nation saw evil!" We truly did experience evil in a way we never had before. Personal evil is much more difficult to deal with than remote or insane evil because it directly touches our lives. The victims of the terrorist attacks, the rescue workers who died in the aftermath, and the grieving loved ones left behind were not strangers across the globe or remote figures from history. They were our fathers and mothers, and our sisters and brothers. They were our children, our grandparents, our coworkers, our neighbors, and our friends. They were not soldiers who willingly risked their lives for a higher cause nor were they casualties caught in the crossfire of political or religious war. They were innocents, going about the daily business of their everyday lives. In one instant they were gone, for reasons we could not easily understand.

In the months that followed the terrorist attacks, there was a sudden explosion of books, articles, and talk shows devoted to the topic of good and evil as Americans wrestled with a host of questions. Are good and evil real? Or are they abstract ideas, relative principles, distinguished only by a difference in degree? How do religious beliefs and morality relate to how we define good and evil? Is "good" truly the nature of God, the divine being who created the universe? Does evil come from God, or is it the result of misguided human action or disobedience?

If evil doesn't originate with God, why does He allow it to exist? Does evil perhaps originate with a real being called Satan, a fallen angel who walks silently behind us, urging us to commit depraved acts of violence? Or, are human beings inherently evil? Is aggression part of our genetic makeup? If so, how will we ever overcome evil?

None of these questions are new. In fact, they have been asked many times throughout human history. What is new is the attention they are receiving, particularly in a literate and secular society that prided itself on the triumph of logic and reason, a society that had long dismissed beliefs in the reality of evil, Satan, and demonic forces. When faced with the personal evil of September 11th, previously held beliefs that minimized the reality of evil and sin were shaken. Interest in good and evil reached an all-time high in this country as people asked the question:

If we are truly created in the image of God,
how can we yet walk in the shadow of demons?

Given the resurgence of evil that now threatened our very way of life, evil did indeed seem real. This confrontation with evil was particularly perplexing for those who held a spiritual view of life that regarded evil as a function of ignorance, error, or even an illusion. This view of life holds that evil was not a part of God's original creation but results from an erroneous perception that is acted upon out of ignorance. Since evil is not a creation of God, it is not real in the sense that it is not eternal.

While evil may not be real in the sense it was not created by God, the **power** of evil is very real and can cause great chaos and destruction. For evil results when we **misapply** our creative abilities in defiance of Divine Will and Universal Law. As co-creators with God, our creative abilities are very potent. We not only have the ability to create worlds, we can also destroy them.

Further, I believe there is another spiritual truth at work that has a bearing upon the evil we see in the world. This is the truth that the physical earth plane is a microcosm of the greater macrocosm of the spiritual universe. What we see on earth is but a reflection of what exists on the spiritual plane. This idea is reflected in the well-known sayings "as above, so below," and "on earth as it is in heaven."

There is a connection between the cosmic forces of good and evil and their manifestations on the earth plane. This connection goes back to the very moment of rebellion by a soul against the Creative Force. It is this moment of rebellion that is the fundamental truth which underlies the stories of the war between the sons of light and the sons of darkness, as told in myths throughout the world.

This is a war that first began on the spiritual plane and was later carried over into the physical world. It is a war waged against spiritual truth by those beings who choose self-interest over the greater good of the human community. It is a war against love, joy, peace, and compassion by those who choose fear, hatred, and anger. It is a war that has been repeatedly played out in the history of humankind by the manipulators of the human body, mind, and spirit. It is this perpetual conflict between good and evil, order and chaos, light and darkness, which was played out once again in the terrorist attacks of September 11, 2001.[1]

Regrettably, the terrorist attacks are likely the first step in what may be the latest phase of this cosmic war as it is played out on the earth plane. Ancient prophecies point to this as a crucial time in human history. It is a time of testing when each soul is being given the opportunity to make the choice to return to the unity of our spiritual source or continue to follow the divisive nature of limited selfish interests. Unity or separation—this is the ultimate choice between good and evil.

We can no longer ignore evil or underestimate its power and influence. Evil is rebellion against the Creative Force. It is the rejection of our true self as a companion and co-creator with God in favor of a false, separate identity. It is a denial of the divine plan of the universe in favor of selfish interests. By minimizing evil, we allow its separation paradigms to flourish and keep humanity chained to a separation consciousness. We perpetuate the erroneous belief of "specialness" that leads to division, dissent, and greed. We accept the lie that tells us we are less than we were created to be.

We must recognize evil for the error it is and take every opportunity to replace error with truth, the truth of who we are and what we were created to be. As companions and co-creators with God, we must choose to "become who we are" and do our part to aid the forces of light in their battle against the darkness. Those who sit on the sidelines and through inaction allow evil to thrive will be lost. The English philosopher Edmond Burke was speaking a great truth when he said,

> "All that is necessary for the triumph of evil
> is for good men to do nothing."

Let us therefore strive always to overcome evil with good.

Kathy L. Callahan
September 2003

Introduction

Nature itself is beyond good and evil
and ignores our egoistic terminology.
Chu Hsi

The Study of Good and Evil

Studies of good and evil, whether by philosophers, priests, or scientists, traditionally concern themselves with similar issues and questions. The first issue that is normally addressed is the distinction between different types of good and evil. Other issues include the relativity of good and evil, universal archetypes, and the paradox of evil.

There are two fundamental types of good and evil: that which is beyond the control of human beings, and that which is the result of human behavior. Impersonal good/evil, also called natural good/evil, refers to those things that originate from sources outside the human condition. It doesn't matter if you believe the driving force behind these manifestations is an impartial universal principle or the will of a divine being. They are beyond human control. Impersonal good/evil encompasses nature phenomena such as weather, rainfall, famine, earthquakes, and drought. Such things as good luck, good health, illness, disease, and death also fall into this category.

Moral good/evil, also called human or psychological good/evil, refers to the good and evil that originate within human nature or more precisely, the human psyche. Moral good and evil may be the result of human action or it can also be the result of human inaction. These are the things we do, or fail to do, to ourselves and to one another. It is the stuff of which the chronicle of human history is made. Moral good includes actions that benefit society as a whole, including self-sacrifice, courage in the face of adversity, and altruism. Moral good also encompasses so-called spiritual attributes such as empathy and compassion. Moral evil encompasses all the cruelties and violence that human beings have inflicted upon one another, or have allowed to be inflicted upon others through indifference and apathy.

The Relativity of Good and Evil

Any study of good and evil must address the fact that from a human viewpoint, our ideas of good and evil are relative and not absolute. What one sees as good and what one sees as evil depends upon the **observer's** viewpoint. This applies to both impersonal and moral good/evil. Two examples follow which illustrate this point. The first concerns impersonal good/evil and is taken from ancient history. The second involves moral good/evil and is based on an incident from our recent past.

The first example occurred over two thousand years ago, when the ancient Greeks were involved in a series of conflicts that came be to known as the Peloponnesian War. The primary antagonists who opposed one another were the Greek city-states of Athens and Sparta. Early in the course of this 30-year war, a plague broke out among the Athenians. The plague decimated a good percentage of the Athenian population and hampered their war effort. The Athenians saw the plague as an evil visited upon them unjustly. The Spartans, however, saw the outbreak of the plague as good, considering it divine retribution for sins their enemy had committed.

The second example is taken from the not too distant past of American history and centers on the actions of General Kit Carson. In the late 1800s, General Carson supplied the Navajo people with food and blankets. The blankets, intended primarily for women and children, had been infected with smallpox. His intent was to destroy the Navajo people by eliminating women of reproductive age and destroying the next generation before it had a chance to reach maturity. He was motivated by a sense of doing good, believing he was acting in the best interests of his country and fellow citizens. To the Navajo, however, this act was nothing short of genocide, a great evil visited upon them by a cruel and merciless enemy.

The point to be made here is that any assessment of good and evil is relative. A determination of what is good and what is evil is based upon two primary factors: the observer's worldview and the observer's personal morality. Worldview refers to the way we perceive ourselves, our relationships with others, and our place in the world. For our purposes, we will recognize two primary viewpoints from which we evaluate good and evil: the "egocentric" view and the "divine" perspective.

The egocentric view stems from a self-view whereby a person analyzes life from his/her (hereafter I will use male/female pronouns interchangeably) own vantage point, putting emphasis only upon his own needs, wants, and concerns. It derives from the ego-self and considers only our own best interests, and not that of others. The divine perspective occurs when a person is able to transcend the self and take into account the needs, wants, and desires of others. The divine perspective derives from the "higher self" or soul-self, and occurs when we view life with spiritual vision. It is the divine view that enables us to make decisions based upon the highest good for all concerned.

There is a story in the Koran, the holy text of Islam, which illustrates the difference between the egocentric viewpoint and the divine perspective. In this story, Moses is traveling with the angel Khidr. As they come upon a village, Khidr sinks the village fishing boats. Moses is upset at this apparent act of evil and complains to Khidr. Khidr informs Moses that bandits were on their way to the village to steal the boats. If he hadn't sunk them, they would have been stolen and the villagers would have lost their means of making a living. By sinking the boats, the villagers only had to raise them from the water and repair them. In this way, Khidr was protecting the villagers' property and ensuring they continued to have the means to engage in their livelihood.

Moses initially saw Khidr's actions as evil. This evaluation was based on Moses' limited egocentric viewpoint. He could not see the larger picture and was judging Khidr's actions according to his own moral values. Khidr, however, was aware of other factors unknown to Moses and was acting according to a divine perspective. Once Moses knew the complete facts of the situation, he saw "the bigger picture" and understood Khidr's actions.

Related to our worldview is our concept of morality. Morality refers to the particular ethics and values we hold to be true. It provides the framework by which we evaluate the world around us. Morality determines our concepts of righteousness and sin and hence influences what we judge as good and what we see as evil.

There is a pitfall, however, in linking the principles of good and evil to concepts of morality. Morality is a humanly determined code of behavior based on **culturally relative value judgments.** As such, our view of morality can change with time, place, and circumstance. As morality changes, so do our perceptions of good and evil. Consider the following scenarios.

Two thousand years ago, a group of Jews was prepared to stone a woman to death because she had been accused of adultery. She was not tried by a jury of her peers nor convicted in court. She was merely accused of adultery. Yet this action was fully justified according to the Jewish religious law of the time. It was also permissible under Roman secular law. Those who planned to stone this woman, as well as those observing the event, considered themselves to be morally justified. Yet how many people today would condone such action?

Seven hundred years ago, the Christian Church pursued a policy of persecution against those accused of having heretical beliefs. People accused of heresy were arrested, imprisoned, and tortured. Many died during the Inquisition's campaign of terror. Such action, however, which often extended to family members, was morally justified under the religious and civic law of the day. Church officials believed they were morally justified in eradicating heresy. Christians today look upon the Inquisition with regret; many would like to forget that it ever happened. Yet happen it did. It remains a "morally justified" scar in the annals of Christian history.

Consider again the actions of General Carson against the Navajo people. Most Americans at that time applauded his actions, believing they were necessary to protect American settlers from future attack by a savage enemy. Today, however, his actions seem comparable to the ethnic cleansing campaigns we so loudly denounce as evil.

As you can see from these examples, morality is human-made, finite, and changeable. Morality varies not only from culture to culture, but will differ over time within the same society. Moreover, an individual's morality can change depending upon his perspective at any moment. Given the fluid nature of morality, it is perhaps not the best yardstick by which to measure good and evil.

The Problem of Evil

Studies of good and evil inevitably end up focusing more on the concept of evil rather than on the concept of good. This is because evil is so difficult to understand. We see and appreciate the value of good but we cannot comprehend the value of evil. We focus on evil because it puzzles us the most. Why does evil exist? How did it come into being? What purpose does it serve? Questions such as these are particularly perplexing for followers of religions based on belief in Jehovah, the all-powerful God of Abraham. The characteristic of absolute being combined with the fundamental goodness of a god who truly loves His children led to a most puzzling paradox. A paradox is a contradiction that occurs when a conclusion, based on a premise known to be true, contradicts common sense. The paradox of evil can be stated as follows: "Why would an omnipotent, all-good God who calls Himself 'our Father' allow evil, impersonal or moral, to be visited upon His children, particularly the innocent?"

The visitation of evil upon the innocent is perhaps the most troubling aspect of this paradox. The underlying premise here is the belief that there is a causal relationship between evil and the commission of a moral offense. Yet we know that there are instances where innocent people who have done nothing immoral are oppressed by evil. This is particularly true in the case of children. Common sense tells us that both premises cannot be true. Therefore, one must be flawed. Since we can see cases where innocents experience evil, the conclusion is that God allows the innocent to suffer. This takes us right back to the original paradox and the cycle of questions starts over again.

In many Eastern religions, the concepts of karma and reincarnation help explain this apparent contradiction. The law of karma is a corollary of the Universal Law of cause and effect. It simply means that every thought you have had, every action you have taken, and every deed you have done will return to you in a similar form. Eastern religions combine the idea of karma with the concept of reincarnation, believing that karma carries over from lifetime to lifetime. This means that the effects we experience in this life may indeed be the result of causes we have enacted in previous incarnations.

While Eastern religions openly embrace the concept of karma, it is less readily recognized by Western religions. It is expressed in Old Testament Scripture as "eye for eye, tooth for tooth, hand for hand, foot for foot" (Exodus 21:24) and in the New Testament as "...for whatever a man sows, that he will also reap." (Galatians 6:7) The Judaic-Christian tradition[2] however, rejected reincarnation and thus had great difficulty explaining why God apparently allowed evil to be visited upon those who had committed no moral offense. The Jewish and Christian responses to the paradox of evil will be addressed in Chapter Two.

A Universal Perspective

It is clear from the preceding discussion that the study of good and evil is a complex issue at best, characterized by a relative subjectivity, and all too often debated with emotion rather than reason. One way to minimize the relative aspects of good and evil is to apply a cross-cultural approach. Used for over a century in anthropological studies, this methodology considers material from a number of cultures, distinctive in time and space. The material is then examined through a comparative analysis that seeks to identify shared themes or patterns, also called archetypes.

Archetypes[3] are universal patterns of feelings, thoughts, and memories shared by humanity. They are the reality that underlies the particular expression we see in the physical world. They give structure, meaning, and value to life experiences. Archetypes are found in mythology, philosophy, religion, psychology, literature, and the arts. Famous archetypes include the Priest, the Old Woman, the Fool, and the Hero.

Archetypes are universal models that incorporate the material, mental, and spiritual aspects of a given principle. They are useful because they help us overcome an egocentric view and understand principles from a universal or divine perspective.

Both good and evil are archetypes. The archetype of Good traditionally embodies the following attributes: order, light, spirit, spiritual truth, intellect, reason, law, and Divine Will. The archetype of Evil embraces their counterparts: chaos, darkness, physical being, ignorance, falsehood, desire, emotion, rebellion, and selfishness. As we continue, you will see that each of these aspects is a fundamental part of what humanity calls good and evil. A more detailed explanation of the archetypes of good and evil is presented in Appendix A.

As a complement to cross-cultural comparison, we will also examine good and evil through the interpretive lens of metaphysics.[4] Metaphysics refers to the branch of philosophy that attempts to understand the fundamental nature of all reality. This includes the material world we perceive with our five physical senses and the unseen world of energy (or spirit) that exists beyond our physical perception. Metaphysics deals with both the nature of existence (ontology) and the systems that regulate existence (cosmology). In lay terms, ontology studies the "who or what" while cosmology deals with the "how." Considered together, they can lead us to the "why."

A metaphysical approach considers an issue from a factual perspective and then evaluates it in terms of symbolic meaning, mental states of consciousness, and spiritual awareness. For this reason, some people consider metaphysics a type of spiritual psychology.[5] A metaphysical lens thus provides a holistic perspective through which we can study the physical, mental, and spiritual aspects of any issue. Like the archetype, a metaphysical lens helps us move beyond an egocentric view and adopt a divine perspective.

Overview

The primary purpose of this book is to help readers come to a more complete understanding of the nature of good and evil (the what), the origin of evil and its place in the universe (the how), and the relationship evil may have to our spiritual development (the why). To achieve this end, we need to understand both principles from the divine perspective. I therefore propose to examine good and evil through cross-cultural study and by means of metaphysical concepts.

The material presented in Part One, Traditional Views of Good and Evil, focuses on the "what" of good and evil. It is thus drawn from a wide selection of philosophies, mythologies, and religious doctrines. We survey the ways good and evil have been defined throughout history, both as abstract principles and as personalized expressions of the divine. We discuss gods, demons, and angels, and explore the historic development of Satan. We also examine the way secular thinkers have described the manifestation of good and evil in human nature.

In Part Two, A Metaphysical View, we turn our focus to the "how" and "why" of evil. In order to do this we must first understand ourselves—who we are, why we were created, and our place in the universe. We will do this from a metaphysical perspective by using the material contained in the Edgar Cayce readings. Those unfamiliar with Cayce's work should refer to Appendix B, which contains a brief synopsis of his life and work. The magnitude of the information contained in 14,000 readings given over 40-plus years makes it one of the best-documented and most consistent sources of psychic information. For that reason alone it warrants consideration. While Christian in orientation, the readings incorporate many Eastern spiritual concepts and thus provide a pan-religious perspective. The readings also provide common sense explanations to many of the difficult questions we will be addressing.

We discuss the expression of good and evil as universal forces and explore the origin of evil as it first appeared in the spiritual dimension and later in the physical world. We also consider the unique idea that Satan is a soul who played a key role in bringing evil into the spiritual and physical planes. We will examine the reality and power of evil and also explore the idea that evil may indeed serve a positive function in our spiritual development. In the final chapter we will apply what we have learned as a means to guide us in making the right choices that will help us oppose evil and overcome it.

The book also includes three appendices that contain additional information on selected subjects. Appendix A presents detailed information on the archetypes of good and evil. Appendix B contains a brief synopsis of Edgar Cayce's life and work. Appendix C contains information about the root races of humankind as presented in the readings.

Part One
Traditional Views of Good and Evil

Over the span of recorded history it was the ancient philosophers who first attempted to define the essence of good and evil and to understand why evil exists. They defined good and evil as absolute concepts that exist independently of human judgment and evaluation. Philosophers often saw good as light, order, reason, nature, and spirit. Evil was the opposite of those qualities, being darkness, chaos, unbridled emotion, irrational thought, and materiality. Good was the ordering principle of all creation while evil resulted from the rejection of that principle.

Some doctrines advocated the principle of monism or one force, meaning that the universe is based upon a single principle or substance. All reality exists as one whole—an undifferentiated unity. While certain aspects of reality appear to be different, such as matter and energy, they are identical at the elemental level of existence. According to this idea, although good and evil may appear to be distinct, they are different expressions of the same principle or force. Examples of monistic philosophies that advocate undifferentiated unity include Taoism and Stoicism.

Other philosophies, however, expressed a belief in dualism. Dualism recognizes two independent and mutually exclusive principles or substances. According to dualism, good and evil are distinct creations that exist independently of one another. They are not different expressions of the same force but direct reflections of two opposing forces. Dualism is expressed in the writings of Plato as Ideas and Forms, and reached its most extreme expression in the Persian religion of Zoroastrianism.

As mythologies developed within human culture, the concepts of good and evil became personified in the form of supernatural beings. These divine beings were often neither good nor evil, but possessed qualities of both. As religious systems of thought developed, good became associated with various gods while evil became associated with beings called demons. Hinduism embraced a pantheon of gods and goddesses while Zoroastrianism expressed the dualistic belief in the existence of two equal and opposing gods—one good and one evil. Although the Judaic-Christian-Islamic traditions upheld the belief in one supreme God, all three religions developed complex demonologies and angelologies.

Western theology focused on moral good/evil, which was defined according to specific belief systems. Good was associated with ideas of righteousness while evil was associated with religiously defined concepts of sin. Impersonal good/evil were considered a direct a correlation of a person's thoughts and actions. Good things happened to good people while bad experiences were reserved for the sinful. Christian teachings in particular advocated that obedience to good principles, as defined by church doctrine, would result not only in a fulfilling life, but also in an eternal spiritual reward. The choice of evil as demonstrated by sinful behavior would lead to dire consequences in this world and the next.

With time, philosophy followed theology's lead as modern philosophers came to view good and evil in terms of righteousness and sin, rather than as abstract concepts. Studies of good and evil fell within the branch of philosophy known as ethics. Ethics focused primarily on the study of the general nature of morals and the specific moral choices to be made by individuals in relationship to others. The goal of ethics, also called "moral philosophy," was to discern the nature of good and evil by making a correlation between these concepts and the goodness or badness of human behavior. The standards of good and evil were now irrevocably linked to culturally relative judgments, often religious in origin, that were dependent upon the fundamental ethics and values of a particular culture.

The advent of the scientific revolution and the rise of humanistic thought actually furthered this process. Good and evil came to be seen as secular moral issues, with good defined as behavior that benefited the civic community. Evil was behavior harmful to society. Many believed that good could be found in the reason of the human mind while evil was attributed to our baser instincts. In the Twentieth Century, scientists debated whether nature (instinct) or nurture (environment) was the most important factor in human behavior.

1
Good and Evil as Cosmic Forces

There is only one good, knowledge,
and only one evil, ignorance.
Socrates

In today's world it is almost impossible to think of the concept of good without associating it with a divine being, be it the God Jehovah, Jesus the Christ, or Allah. It is equally difficult for many people to hear the word "evil" without associating it with a satanic spirit or demon. Christians in particular tend to think of evil as directly related to a demonic being called Satan, popularly known as the Devil. The reason for this personal association is that many religions conceive of the divine in terms of a personal being having the same qualities and characteristics we see within ourselves.

Yet long before the concept of the divine became personified in the form of gods and demons, our ancestors saw the divine as abstract principle. As such, it had no personal qualities but existed within and beyond all physical form. Good and evil were not entities in their own right but part of the world order.

An extreme form of the impersonal divine was known as pantheism, which is the belief that the divine exists in everything. The divine was seen as the origin of all being and an integrated part of all creation. This idea, called divine immanence, holds that the divine and the world are thus identical. Since the divine existed in all creation it did not possess individuality.

At the other end of the spectrum, the concept of the impersonal divine found its most abstract expression in the Mahayana order of Buddhism. Nagarjuna, a Second Century monk, conceived of the divine originating principle as the ultimate transcendence of all being and thought. This was so far beyond human understanding that it could only be described as a void or "Nothingness" of existence, lacking any personal or finite characteristics.

A familiar modern day expression of the idea of the impersonal divine is the concept of "the Force," popularized by the *Star Wars* movies. Ben Kenobi, a wise sage, teaches his pupil Luke Skywalker about the Force, defining it as "an energy field created by all living things. It surrounds us and penetrates us. It binds the galaxy together."[6] Through attunement with the Force, an individual can attain knowledge and master powers and abilities that overcome the limitations of the physical world.

The existence of a vital life force or energy that permeated all of creation has been universally acknowledged since ancient times. This force was believed to exist in all things, living and nonliving. The Hindus called this force *prana*, the Chinese called it *qi* or *chi*, while the Japanese termed it *ki*. Although there was no one word for this force among Native American cultures, most tribes in North America believed in its existence. The people of Oceania referred to this essence as *mana*. Anthropologists adopted this Melanesian word as a generic term for this concept.

The Mana Concept of Early Cultures

Mana was generally regarded as a basic element of the universe. It was the source of all energy, force, and power. Mana was present in all things external to the earth as well as all things upon the earth. The sun, moon, and stars possessed mana, as did all people, animals, plants, and inanimate objects. Depending upon the cultural tradition, mana was thought to flow through humans in waves, layers, or circular patterns that converged at focal points in the body. We know these today as the meridians of traditional Chinese medicine and the chakras of Hindu tradition.

While mana existed in all aspects of creation, some beliefs held that mana energy would gravitate to certain areas or objects, such as a mountaintop or sites of running water. Perhaps this is why these locales later became associated with divine beings, such as Mount Olympus—the home of the Greek gods, Mount Sinai—where the God Jehovah spoke to Moses, and the sacred pool of the ancient Oracle of Delphi. Similarly, people who possessed high levels of mana were believed to be those who manifested good health, great strength, or even magic powers. Conversely, illness was associated with a depleted level of mana energy. The curative powers of healers were attributed to their ability to harness mana and transfer it to the diseased person. The Christian tradition of healing through the "laying on of hands" actually derives from this belief.

To our ancestors, mana was neither good nor evil. Mana simply was. It existed as an impartial and uncontrollable force that was a part of all life. Rituals were designed to increase a person's level of mana. In Eastern cultures, these rituals centered on the mastery of mana flow within the body and focused on breath control, meditation, and yoga practices. In other areas of the world, these rituals aimed at harnessing the mana that existed in the outer world. Self-deprivation, mutilation, and induced states of altered consciousness, either through drugs or other means, were used in rituals designed to break down the barriers between humans and the natural world so they might access the mana that existed in nature. The vision quest, common to some native North American cultures, is one such ritual that has lasted into modern times. Those who were successful at harnessing and controlling high levels of mana were distinguished from others; they were the priests, the medicine men, and the shaman.

As the rites for controlling mana became more codified, mana began to take on aspects of good and evil. However, "good" mana or "bad" mana were thought to derive not from the essence of mana itself, but from the **intentions** of the person harnessing its power. Those who used its power for good were the priests and healers mentioned above. Those who used its power for evil were labeled sorcerers, witches, or other terms. Yet even though certain people were recognized as being able to control and manipulate mana for varying ends, the mana force itself continued to be thought of as an impersonal and neutral power.

The Way of Tao

The writings of the *Tao Te Ching* are attributed to Lao-Tzu, a Sixth Century B.C.E. Chinese philosopher. They represent some of humanity's earliest writings and teach the existence of an eternal, impersonal, and unifying principle that governs all existence. This principle is called Tao, the eternal way. Only Tao remains constant. All other things change and transform. Attachment to material things is senseless since they never remain the same. Once we understand the impermanence of material things, we come to value the way of Tao as the only constant in our lives. We achieve harmony by following the natural currents of Tao.

Taoist philosophy consists of three doctrines. The first, Tao, the way, is nonbeing or *wu*. It is the creative force that brings all creation into being and then in turn dissolves everything into nonbeing. The second doctrine is return or *fu*, the destiny of all existence. All forms of creation, after completing their cycle, will return to nonbeing. Nonaction or *wu wei* is the third doctrine and refers to action that is in harmony with nature. This is considered to be the best way of life.

Chuang-tzu, a Third Century B.C.E. philosopher, taught that freedom from the bondage of the physical world was the keynote of Tao. Since Tao, the way of nature, is in a constant state of flux, one must be free of all connections with the material world in order to discover one's true being. A true understanding of Tao came not from traditional schooling that emphasized the material life, but through the experience of life itself. Discovery of Tao and adherence to its way of harmony is achieved through the practice of balance, restraint, simplicity, avoidance of activity, and elimination of desire. A long and tranquil life is thus achieved by the elimination of one's desires and aggressive emotions.

According to Taoism, all opposites, including good and evil, are simply different points of conceptual thought and do not possess any real intrinsic value. From a purely objective viewpoint, good is no more preferable than evil. The wise person understands this and accepts the inevitable changes of life as they occur. The following story provides an excellent example of this line of Taoist thinking. It has been retold many times in varying forms.

There was a farmer who found a horse in his pasture. "Ah, such good fortune you now have a horse to plow your fields," said his neighbor. "Perhaps, we shall see," said the farmer.

The following day the farmer's son was riding the horse. The horse tripped upon a stone and fell, crushing the young man's leg. "Ah, such bad fortune that your son broke his leg," said the neighbor. "Perhaps, we shall see," replied the farmer.

The next week the army came to the village looking for young men to conscript into service. Since the young man's leg was broken, the army did not take him. "Ah, such good fortune for your son," said the neighbor. "Perhaps, we shall see," retorted the farmer.

That night, while the farmer was away, there was a terrible storm and lightning struck a large tree beside the farmer's house. The tree instantly split in two and fell upon the house, killing the young man as he slept in his bed. Upon hearing this news, the neighbor went to console the farmer. "Ah such evil fortune, my dear friend, to lose your son." "Perhaps," said the farmer. "We shall see..."

This marvelous short story illustrates the way of Tao, and shows how all things are relative when considered within the constant flux of change. Good and evil are one and the same. They are simply different expressions of the changing currents of Tao.

The Logos of Stoicism

Like Taoism, the Stoicism of the ancient Greeks was based upon a belief in an impersonal and unifying principle of the world that regulates an ever-changing cosmos. The word "logos" derives from the Greek verb *lego*, meaning, to say or to reason. By the classical Greek period it had taken on a variety of other meanings including rational principle, reason, and argument. While the Tao of Chinese philosophy had an almost mystical quality to it, the Logos concept of Stoicism clearly defines this ultimate principle as a rational and regulating principle, responsible for the order and harmony of the cosmos.

One of the first to use the concept of Logos was

Heraclitus of Ephesus, circa 480 B.C.E. To Heraclitus, all creation was ever-changing. Nothing was static. All change occurred according to a fixed and unalterable law that is the basic principle governing the universe.

> "This *one* [italics for author's emphasis] order of things, neither any one of the gods nor men has made, but it always was, is, and ever shall be, an ever-living fire, kindling according to fixed measure and extinguished according to fixed measure."[7]

Heraclitus used the term Logos to refer to the immanent, rational principle that governed the universe through the imposition of relation and order. As a part of the universe, humankind was subject to this law. The universal Logos was represented on the physical level by human thought, reason, and discourse, which imposed a natural ordering upon the ever-changing world. Logos is thus seen as divine in the sense that it governs all things. Yet it is also ordinary in the sense that it is something we encounter each day.

Believing the cosmos to be comprised of one principle, Heraclitus saw good and evil as two notes of the same harmony. He was one of the first thinkers to propose that those things that seem to be opposite in nature are actually one and the same. His famous example is ice and water. Ice which is hard, changes into water, which is soft. They appear to be different substances but they are truly the same.

From here he hypothesized that just as music is composed of high and low notes, so the one harmony and ordering of the universe is composed of opposites. Humankind sees only the opposites and thinks them different. God sees the harmony and knows them to be one, part of the whole. Heraclitus taught that good was living life in harmony with the divine reason of Logos.

Evil, often viewed as a rejection of reason, was simply another note of the universal harmony, a necessary part of the whole.

The Logos concept was adopted by the philosophical movement of Stoicism, founded by Zeno of Citium in the Third Century B.C.E. To the Stoics, the universe consisted of two essences: force, an active principle that moves and acts, and matter, that which is acted upon.

Rather than seeing these as separate, however, the Stoics saw force and matter as united. They believed that the ever-changing element of fire was the substance from which air, water, earth, and all other elements arose. These elements combined in many ways to form the "soul of the universe." This active principle of force, or Logos, was a divine, intelligent force that brought the universe into existence. As universal reason,[8] it permeates and orders all creation.

The early Stoics of Greece incorporated Heraclitus' ideas with the austere philosophy of Zeno that maintained the highest good lay in obedience to the reason and logic of Logos. Since Logos existed within all things, humans possessed the reason of Logos and could learn the law of Logos through the analytic faculties of the mind. The goal of each person was to use the faculty of reason to discover her place in the Divine Order and live according to the dictates of reason. Good was therefore defined as knowing one's place in the universal harmony and living according to the laws of reason. By doing this, a person achieved true happiness, which inevitably results from good.

Humans also possessed the faculty of choice, however, and could disregard the dictates of reason in favor of emotion. Emotions and passions led to false judgments, the rejection of reason, and brought about disharmony and chaos, which was reflected in the world as evil. Evil was not real in the sense that it existed separately. Rather, it was viewed as friction within the harmony of the universal order.

During the period of Roman Stoicism, the concepts of good and evil took on a moral imperative. This was due in part to the fact that Roman Stoics emphasized their beliefs as a way of life rather than mere rhetoric. Lucius Seneca, one of the most influential Roman Stoics, taught that the truly good person was one who learned to control his emotions, and could not be shaken by the whims of fortune, be they pleasant or ill.

The Roman Stoics further believed that the practice and application of Stoic principles was to extend from the level of the individual to the level of the state. Since all people shared in the divine Logos through the faculties of the mind, all were members of a cosmic society governed by the ordering of the natural laws of Logos.

The highest expression of good, therefore, was to be found in the promotion of good law, civic duty, social responsibility, and the equal rights of all human beings. In fact, the Roman Empire was the first government to grant citizenship and rights to conquered peoples. The practical application of Roman Stoicism at the state level, combined with the Stoic belief in a universal brotherhood of humankind, was to have a great impact upon modern thought.

The Dualism of Plato

The Greek philosopher Plato, 428-347 B.C.E., is acknowledged as one of the greatest thinkers of all time. Born to a prestigious Athenian family he held political ambition until the trial and suicide of his teacher and friend Socrates, another renowned Greek philosopher. Following Socrates' death, Plato left Athens and traveled widely throughout the Middle East. Occult lore maintains that while in Egypt, Plato was initiated into an ancient mystery religion in a subterranean hall of the

Great Pyramid.[9]   Indeed, Plato's emphasis on the eternal aspect of the soul and the impermanent nature of the physical world, along with mythological references in his writings, indicate he was well versed in the teachings of the ancient Greek mystery religions. He eventually returned to Athens and in 387 B.C.E. established the Academy, the first university where students could explore all fields of knowledge.

It is through Plato's writings[10] that the ideas of Socrates have survived. It is difficult to say how much of Plato's writings can be directly attributed to Socrates and how much originated with Plato. His writings come to us in the form of "dialogues" because Plato believed that discussion was the best way a student could learn. The key figure in the dialogues is the elder Socrates.

The concept of the universe found in Platonic philosophy is based on dualism. To Plato, all that exists in the universe can be explained through the two concepts of being and becoming. The real world existed in the realm of Ideas or Forms,[11] the ordering principle of the universe.   Forms were not created but have always existed in a perfect state, independent of all things.   Forms are in a state of being, changeless, objective, and eternal; they are therefore real. They are the primary archetypes or original blueprints from which the material world derives its structure.

The physical world of matter is the raw material upon which Forms are impressed. The objects we experience in the physical world are reflections of these external patterns.   Matter is in a constant process of change; it is therefore unreal or illusory. The physical world we experience through the five physical senses is not real but a shadow world of the true reality of Forms.

Plato used the analogy of a sculptor to explain this concept. The sculptor visualizes an idea of a figure he wishes to reproduce in the substance of marble. The idea itself is independent of the marble and would exist even if the marble did not. The sculptor impresses the idea upon the marble thereby creating a copy of the original Form. In Plato's *Dialogues*, he refers to a "demiurge" who impressed the world of Forms upon matter, thereby creating the physical world we experience. Plato does not further define the demiurge nor explain how Form and matter were created. They simply existed at the moment of creation.

Plato believed that man's ability to know both Form and matter derived from the fact that human beings are a unique creation consisting of three aspects: reason, will, and appetites. During creation, the Form of (divine) Reason was impressed upon the matter of the human body. Reason is an archetypal Form, a transcendent intelligence that orders all existence in accordance with the wisdom of the highest Form—Good. Plato often compared Good to the sun, for just as the physical sun enables growth, Good enables us to achieve rational illumination—Reason. Through Reason humankind could order life according to Good, and thus bring about wisdom and happiness. Opposed to Reason was an element of irrationality called Necessity, associated with matter and instinctual desire. Necessity expressed itself in humanity as the physical appetites. Through the will, the spiritual part of man concerned with right action, humans choose to exercise Reason or to obey the dictates of physical desires, appetites, and passions.

In the Platonic universe, therefore, good was seen as living a life where Reason was exercised through the will to rule the appetites. Evil resulted from a failure to exercise Reason, which then allowed the appetites to dominate one's actions. The expression of good and evil in earthly terms were both reflections of higher archetypal Forms. Good was seen as the exercise of Reason and the Idea of the Good, which brought discipline and order. The expression of evil was the failure to exercise Reason, thereby allowing Necessity and its irrationality to dominate.

Many of the ideas contained in Plato's writings did not necessarily originate with him, and can in fact be found in older philosophies, as well as in Eastern religious and philosophical teachings. He was the first, however, to record his views in writings that have survived to modern times. For this reason, the ideas of Plato have had a lasting impact upon the development of Western philosophical and religious thought.

2
Good and Evil Personified

No one can study chemistry and see the wonderful way
in which certain elements combine with the nicety
of the most delicate machine ever invented,
and not come to the inevitable conclusion that
there is a Big Engineer who is running this universe.
Thomas Edison

In the last chapter we discussed good and evil as impersonal principles or forces. The association of good and evil with supernatural beings as portrayed in mythology and religion does not contradict the idea of good and evil as abstract principles. Rather, the personalization of good and evil in the form of divine beings complements our understanding of the many ways in which good and evil are expressed in the material world.

The Role of Mythology

Supernatural beings have their origin in mythic tradition. A mythic tradition is a set of related, symbolic stories designed to answer questions of life and death. Myths explain the origin of the world, humanity's creation, and provide reasons for the appearance of natural phenomena. These stories give meaning and order to life on a personal and cultural level. It was here, in the mythic traditions, that the concepts of good and evil became associated with gods and goddesses and began to be described in terms of personal behavior.

The oldest forms of mythic deities find their beginnings in the expressions of earth and sky. This is likely a consequence of the mana concept of early cultures, whereby the divine force of mana was thought to concentrate in various geographic and celestial locations.

The sky was often perceived as masculine while the earth was considered female. In some mythic traditions, such as Mesopotamian and Native American myths, the union of father sky and mother earth resulted in the birth of new deities. These deities were often associated with thunder, lightning, and rain, or with nature phenomena such as mountains, water, and trees. Some deities appeared as cultural heroes who brought knowledge and invention to the human race.

In the great mythic traditions of the Greeks, Romans, Celts, and Norsemen, deities were described in terms of personal characteristics and behavior. These mythic traditions are similar in that the divine beings portrayed in them were neither entirely good nor evil, but possessed characteristics of both. Each god or goddess was associated with a certain realm, such as earth, sky, and ocean, or a quality such as love, war, and knowledge. No one deity was depicted as being purely good or purely evil. In fact, the gods and goddesses portrayed in mythic sagas possessed the same emotions and passions as humans. Myths are filled with stories of love, hate, jealousy, and wrath, whose ebb and flow depended on the deities' desires. These gods and goddesses are really reflections of humanity, with all its virtues and vices.[12]

Since mythic traditions developed to explain the existence of phenomena in the world around us, some myths tried to address the origin of evil. One of the earliest recorded attempts to explain the existence of evil in the world is found in the Greek legend of Pandora. Pandora, the first human woman, was created by Zeus to plague mankind in retaliation for its acceptance of Prometheus' gift of fire, which he had stolen from the heavens and presented to mortals. Zeus endowed Pandora with charm, beauty, and curiosity, and then presented her with a box, instructing her never to open it. Curiosity got the best of her and she pried it open. As she did so, all the evils, troubles, and diseases the world now knows were released. The legend goes on to say that she managed to close the lid in time to prevent hope from escaping. Humankind, therefore, still has hope. In Greek mythology, therefore, the origin of evil is linked with disobedience to the will of a god. The evils of the world can be traced first to Prometheus' disobedient act, then to humanity's acceptance of Prometheus' gifts, in defiance of Zeus' will, and finally to the disobedient act of a curious woman.

From Myth to Religion

With the development of a literate class, theology came to replace myth as the foundation of religious belief. The term "theology" is taken from the Greek words *theos* meaning god, and *logos,* meaning reason. It was first coined by Plato who used it to refer to a rational conception of the divine as opposed to poetic myths and sagas. It is well recognized today that our conception of the divine is rarely based on logic and reason, but derives from religious traditions based on faith and rooted in divine revelation. Theology, however, is more than a body of religious beliefs. It implies a reasoned and logical understanding of those beliefs, even though the belief itself may be based upon mystic revelation and accepted through faith.

There are two major types of theologies: polytheism, which is the belief in many gods, and monotheism, which is the belief in one supreme being. In polytheism, gods are personified, distinguished by function, and often related to one another in a cosmic family. The deities of polytheistic religions often took on the characteristics of good **or** evil, sometimes displaying characteristics of both. Hinduism is the principal polytheistic religion in existence today, although it is based on a monistic philosophy. In monotheistic religions, the supreme being is usually characterized as a transcendent being who is omnipotent and omniscient. Judaism, Christianity and Islam, which share a common ancestry, are the primary monotheistic religions. Zoroastrianism, the religion of ancient Persia, began as a monotheistic religion that later took on aspects of polytheism. It is distinguished by an extreme form of dualism whereby the forces of good and the forces of evil are locked in a perpetual battle.

The Beliefs of Hinduism

Hinduism developed over a period of 4,000 years, and has no single founder or creed. It consists of a variety of beliefs and practices that include six different philosophical systems and two major theistic movements—the cult of Vishnu and the cult of Shiva. The Hindu belief system is further complicated by the fact that Hinduism grew out of an earlier religion called Vedism. Vedism, from a Sanskrit word meaning knowledge, represents the religious thought of the Aryans who invaded India in the second millennium B.C.E. Vedic beliefs are expressed in the *Vedas*, a collection of four hymns that represent the oldest literature of India, and are considered the most sacred books of Hinduism. Vedism emphasizes a belief in a blissful future existence in heaven and the performance of sacrificial fire rituals to various nature deities in order to achieve desired results on earth that reflect heavenly existence. Vedism lacked the concepts of karma, rebirth, and liberation from the karmic cycle, which first appeared in the *Upanishads* and played a central role in later Hindu beliefs. The major gods of later Hinduism, principally Shiva and Vishnu, trace their origins to the minor deities of the Vedas.

Because of its unique development, Hinduism combines elements of different philosophical beliefs with religious symbolism. The polytheistic pantheon of Hindu gods and goddesses is actually built upon a monistic belief in the universal nature of pure being or Brahman.

In earlier pantheistic beliefs, Brahman was universal principle, the origin of all creation and the infinite reality behind the illusory and imperfect world of human perception. According to this philosophy, only Brahman, the universal, supreme, pure, and good being, and *atman*, the individual self, are real. Brahman and atman are in fact, identical. However, *avidya* or ignorance prevents the individual self from understanding the true nature of Brahman. Through ignorance we experience the illusion that the material world (*maya*) is separate from Brahman. The limits of sensory perception prevent us from realizing that this is an illusion. Evil, as a part of the phenomenal world, is illusion and therefore not real.

Hinduism also holds that the universe is populated by a multitude of major and minor deities and numerous other intelligences such as demigods, spirits, and attendants. Hindu polytheism is organized under a trinity of primary deities: Brahma, the Immense Being, Vishnu, the Redeemer, and Shiva, the Destroyer or Transformer. Shakti, an all-pervading or divine Energy, has also been portrayed as a great goddess since early times. Other major gods include Ganesha (god of overcoming obstacles), Kali (goddess of the power of time), Lakshmi (fortune), and Parvati (peaceful energy). The complexity of Hindu cosmology makes it impossible to address all the varied aspects of good and evil as reflected in the many Hindu deities. However, we can examine a few of the basic Hindu beliefs regarding good and evil.

The trinity of Brahma-Vishnu-Shiva clearly reflects the good as order-chaos as evil analogy common to many philosophies. Brahma is viewed as the creative aspect of the Hindu trinity. He is responsible for creating the world at the beginning of each new cycle of existence. Vishnu, the Redeemer, is seen as the preserver and protector of the world. Through his actions he brings order and discipline to humanity, and is responsible for the reordering of the world following each period of cyclic creation. Shiva, the Destroyer, is the god who brings about the cyclic dissolution of the world. Shiva, however, is not viewed as a purely evil god but is portrayed in both terrible and graceful forms.

This dual depiction of Shiva is due to the fact that he is associated with the advent of chaos, which in the Hindu belief system is not considered evil at an elemental level. While chaos is initially viewed through human perception as evil, it also has a transforming quality that can lead to a state of growth and enlightenment.   The idea of chaos possessing a transforming quality can be traced back to the Vedic tradition of Brahman, where chaos is a different expression of the infinite whole of reality or Brahman.

As a monistic philosophy, Hinduism does not embrace the idea of absolute good and absolute evil. Good and evil are viewed as a difference in degree of spiritual development, rather than as independent states or powers. Stages of development that we have yet to encounter are seen as angelic and good. They are represented by divinities or *devas*, Sanskrit for "the shining ones." Their purpose is to further our spiritual development by helping us break the karmic cycle of earthly lives. Stages of development that we have left behind are seen as a hindrance to spiritual progress and appear as dark and evil. These are represented by the antigods or *asura*, whose role is to entangle us once again in karmic debt and hinder our spiritual enlightenment. Thus Hinduism, while being a polytheistic religion, takes a monistic view of good and evil, seeing them as a difference in degree rather than in kind.

The Opposition of Good and Evil in Zoroastrianism

The radical dualism of Zoroastrianism had no problem explaining the existence of evil because it saw good and evil as two independent and opposing forces, both created at the time of creation. These two forces were locked in perpetual battle in the spiritual and material worlds.

In the Seventh Century B.C.E., a prophet known as Zoroaster reformed the polytheistic religion of the ancient Persians, which shared similar origins with Hinduism. Its theology and cosmology would later influence the development of Greek, Jewish, Christian, and Muslim thought. As a result of this reform movement, Ahura Mazda, one of the divine *ahura* (lord), was elevated to the position of the one true God from whom all other deities received their being. Other ahuras took on aspects of the goodness of Ahura Mazda. The gods and demigods referred to as devas in the Hindu Vedic tradition were demonized and took on aspects of evil. These conflicting forces of good and evil continually opposed one another on both the spiritual and material planes.

According to Zoroaster, the god Ahura Mazda, the Wise Lord of Good and Light, was the sole creator of the world and all that was good. Ahura Mazda fathered twin sons, the "twin spirits," who possessed the gift of free will. The first of these, Spenta Mainyu or Bounteous Spirit, used his will to further the goodness of his father. The other, Angra Mainyu or Hostile Spirit, used his free will to oppose goodness and create destructive evil. The Bounteous Spirit was aided by the ahuras or lesser gods of Persia: Good Mind, Truth, Right Mindedness, Dominion, Health, and Life. Hostile Spirit, who was later called Ahriman, was aided by six major devas: Evil Mind, Warfare, Tyranny, Arrogance, Hunger, and Thirst.

After Zoroaster's death, Ahura Mazda and his son Bounteous Spirit came to be seen as one being, the supreme God or Wise Lord, responsible for all life and goodness in the world. Ahriman, the Hostile Spirit, came to be seen as an opponent of the Wise Lord himself rather than a lesser force of evil. He became a co-eternal enemy of the Wise Lord who stood separate and opposed to him since the beginning of time. Hence, the monotheistic concept of God that was intended by Zoroaster developed into a theology of radical dualism.

In the dualistic world of Zoroastrianism, good and evil are considered separate principles, personified in the form of Ahura Mazda and Ahriman, respectively. Evil, therefore, did not present a problem to Zoroastrianism, for it was viewed as an independent principle and substance that existed apart from the good God. All good came from the Wise Lord Ahura Mazda. All evil and suffering came from his opponent Ahriman, the god of evil and destruction.

In an attempt to deceive humankind, Ahriman created "the Lie," which is the belief that evil comes from Ahura Mazda rather than from himself. Ahriman hoped that by believing the Lie, humanity would reject the ways of Ahura Mazda and follow him on a path of ever increasing evil and destruction. The ahuras, lead by Bounteous Spirit, always choose good and aid humankind. The devas, on the other hand, believe the Lie taught by Ahriman and take action to further his cause. They are many in number and are known as the demons of ruin, pain, and vileness.

At the time of creation, it was revealed that the battle between good and evil must be won by good. This result was inevitable since both the body and the soul were created by Ahura Mazda. They belong to him and must therefore eventually return to him and take up the cause of good. Because of this, Ahura Mazda had already won; Ahriman had lost and would eventually be destroyed.

The conflict between good and evil is thus finite and is destined to end in the destruction of Ahriman and the evil he created. All human souls will eventually recognize the evil deception of Ahriman and return to Ahura Mazda, the source of all good and wise creation.

The Judaic-Christian Tradition

The three major religions of Western civilization, Judaism, Christianity, and Islam, share roots in Middle Eastern history and mythology. All three honor the text of the Old Testament as divine revelation and believe in "the one true god" who first revealed himself to Abraham and later to Jacob, Isaac, and Moses. He was addressed in the Old Testament as Yahweh or Jehovah. He is absolute, omnipotent, and omniscient. He not only created the universe but also continues to take an active role in its operation.

A parallel belief holds that because the world was created and governed by a single mind, it is intelligible and purposeful; everything has meaning. The key to understanding lies in divine revelation as revealed by God to His representatives or prophets. The commandments were given to God's people so that they might regulate their lives and live in accordance with Divine Will, thus becoming a harmonious part of the universe.

The god of ancient Israel is referred to by many names in the Bible, the principal being Yahweh, which likely derives from the Hebrew letters YHWH, and translates to "I AM THAT I AM." This name was first revealed to Moses from the burning bush (see Exodus 3:14). The name Jehovah is most probably an English corruption of the Hebrew translation.

The very name of God itself, I AM THAT I AM, shows that Jewish theology conceived of Yahweh in abstract terms. In Jewish Kabbalah teachings, God is defined as the immutable totality of all existence, so all-encompassing as to be unintelligible to the finite human mind.

Yet a quick review of the Old Testament will show that the God of Israel is also portrayed in personal terms. He is portrayed as a God that wishes to be known by those He calls "my people." Genuine knowledge of God comes through the process of revelation, whereby the deity takes the initiative and unveils holy mysteries so the human mind can understand them. Knowledge of God is personal and implies a relationship of mutual trust and respect. Biblical metaphors, which describe the personal aspects of God, include strength, majesty, eternity, protective watchfulness, patronage, shield, rock, father, redeemer, judge, and shepherd.

God speaks with Adam and Eve in the Garden of Eden. He warns Noah of the destruction a great flood will bring. He speaks with Abraham and makes a covenant with him and his descendants. He literally wrestles with Abraham's grandson Jacob. He appears to Moses in the guise of a burning bush, instructs him to lead the Israelite people out of Egyptian bondage, and then empowers him so he can carry out that plan. He becomes angry when, shortly after being freed from the bondage of Egypt, the people make a golden calf and worship the idol. When they repent, He forgives. He repeatedly forgives David for his transgressions and promises that from his house will come the savior of the world. In fact, the Psalms of King David depict his relationship with a very personal God, a God of love, forgiveness, mercy, and hope.

In the New Testament, Jesus of Nazareth reaffirms this personal concept of God when he addresses Him as "Abba." This word denotes a very familiar form of father, similar to the English "dad." Thus, the omnipotent, absolute, all encompassing I AM THAT I AM which transcends all physical boundaries is also the very personal Lord, Adonai, heavenly Father, Abba.

The Paradox of Good and Evil

It is the very characteristic of absolute being combined with the fundamental goodness of a god who truly loves his "children" that makes the concept of evil so difficult to explain in the Judaic-Christian-Islamic tradition. The question addressed within the framework of these religions was why the God who called Himself "our Father" would allow evil to be visited upon His children, particularly the innocent who had apparently done nothing wrong. This question set up a paradox that would concern theologians for centuries to come.

The Jewish Point of View:
Evil as a Result of Disobedience to God

Jewish theology dealt with the question of evil by considering it a consequence of disobedience to God's law, a breaking of the covenant God had established with Abraham and his descendants. In Exodus 24:7 we read that Moses took "the book of the covenant, and read it in the hearing of the people; and they said 'All that the Lord has spoken we will do, and we will be obedient.'" So long as the people of Israel were obedient to Yahweh's commandments, they would enjoy His blessings.

On the national level, the indignities of foreign domination and forced exile experienced by the Israelites were thought to be consequences of earlier disobedience to God's ways. On an individual level, illness and misfortune were believed to be the result of a person's violation of a commandment, or even the harboring of disobedient thoughts. Evil was not an external force arbitrarily visited upon people, but a result of God's divine justice.

The concept of evil as a consequence of opposition to God is found throughout the Old Testament. The Genesis story describes not only humankind's creation, but gives a detailed account of how humanity's future was forever altered through disobedience. This occurred when Adam and Eve, contrary to God's command, ate of the Tree of Knowledge. Because of their disobedient actions, Adam and Eve were expelled from the Garden of Eden, where all their needs had been met, and compelled to roam the earth. They were thereafter destined to toil in sorrow until they returned to the dust of the earth from which they were made. Their act of disobedience, or "original sin" was believed to be the source of the evils that would befall humanity throughout the centuries.

Similarly, only faithful Noah and his family were saved during the Biblical flood which destroyed a disobedient and rebellious humanity. When Sodom and Gomorrah were destroyed, only the righteous Lot and his family were saved. For generations, the fortunes of the kings of Israel and Judah rose and fell depending upon whether they obeyed the word of the Lord or abandoned His teachings. The prophet Ezekiel believed that Yahweh used the Babylonian empire to punish the Israelites for the worship of other gods.

The continued suffering of the Israelites in the face of their return to God's ways was mitigated by the belief in Old Testament messianic prophecies that stated virtue and obedience would be rewarded at the end of time when God would send a Messiah to redeem His people. The oppression of Jewish culture during the expansion of Greek influence in the Second Century B.C.E. resulted in a heightened interest in messianism, and led to the appearance of Jewish apocalyptic writings. These writings foretold of a final conflict between the forces of good and evil at the end of time. Emphasis on messianic and apocalyptic prophecies of the Old Testament intensified in the First Century B.C.E. when Jewish political independence was ended by Roman rule. Christianity had its beginnings as one of these messianic-apocalyptic movements.

The Christian Response

The paradox of good and evil proved to be a particularly perplexing issue for Christianity because it admitted the existence of an omnipotent, omniscient, and benevolent God and yet acknowledged the real and independent existence of evil. Christian theologians and philosophers struggled with these apparent contradictions during the early development of Christianity. It was St. Augustine, however, who formulated what was to become the official Christian solution to the problem of evil.

St. Augustine, 354-430 C.E. was perhaps the greatest philosopher-theologian of the early Christian church. He also had a profound impact on the subsequent development of Western thought and culture. He received a Roman education in the classics and in his early life adopted Manicheanism,[13] a Gnostic, dualistic religion of Persian origin, which was based on a rational Christianity of strict celibacy and ascetic practices. After nine years he abandoned Manicheanism, disillusioned by their strict practices. He then turned to Neoplatonic literature, a philosophy that combined classical Greek philosophy with Christian beliefs. A short time later he experienced a dramatic conversion. This led him to devote his life to the pursuit of spiritual truth, which he now identified with Christianity.

St. Augustine repeatedly defended the Church against the attacks of separatist movements that sought to divide the early Christian community. In his writings he emphasized unity as the hallmark of true Christianity. He stressed that the original sin of Adam and Eve extended to all their descendants and thus prevented anyone from controlling his own motivation. It was only through God's grace that a person could will to do good. All were therefore equal in God's eyes, and could not be set apart on the grounds of religious exclusivism or moral worth. His philosophy unified many elements of Christianity and emerged as the dominant theology of medieval Europe.

St. Augustine's response to the questions raised by the good-evil paradox combined dualistic ideas with Platonic concepts. This is not so surprising, however, if you consider his past as a Manichean and his familiarity with Neoplatonism.

St. Augustine made a distinction between two types of evil. These were natural evil, meaning a catastrophic event of some kind, and moral evil, meaning evil committed by humanity. Like Plato, he argued that natural evil does not exist in itself but is an imperfect reflection of the real, which is good. The influence of Stoic ideas is reflected in his statement that evil is not really evil from God's point of view. We perceive something as evil because we evaluate it with our limited and finite vision and not the eternal vision and knowledge of God.

St. Augustine differed from Plato and the Stoics, however, in that he defined moral evil as real. Moral evil was not created by God but by Satan, who chose to reject his true nature as an angel and desired instead to be as God. His concept of moral evil as real reflects the dualistic ideas of Manicheanism. St. Augustine goes on to say that moral evil entered the world through the original sin of Adam and Eve, who at Satan's prompting ate the forbidden fruit of the Tree of Knowledge. By doing this, they rejected their true nature as creations of God and sought instead to become as God.

The Christian church quickly adopted St. Augustine's views on the nature of evil because they explained the existence of evil while maintaining the omnipotence and benevolence of God. Satan introduced evil into creation through the sin of pride. Evil was not a part of creation but a deprivation of the original state of good brought about by God's own creations. Humanity had brought moral evil upon itself through the exercise of free will. God, however, would not interfere with the exercise of the free will of His children, even if that meant the propagation of evil in the world.

3
Of Angels and Demons

With the bringing into creation the manifested forms,
there came that which has been, is, and ever will be,
the spirit realm and its attributes—
designated as angels and archangels.
Edgar Cayce Reading 5749-3

In the world's major religions, the personification of good and evil in the form of supreme deities extended to a host of lesser beings subject to the will of the greater gods. Detailed descriptions of spiritual hierarchies of both good and evil beings can be found in all of today's major religions including Hinduism, Judaism, Zoroastrianism, Christianity, and Islam. The forces of light, which brought goodness and order to humanity, came to be known as angels while the forces of darkness that visited evil and chaos upon the world were called demons.

Angelic Expressions of Good

An angel is a celestial being, superior to mortal man but subordinate to God. Angels act as agents or messengers by carrying messages from God to humankind. The Hebrew word for angel is *malakh*, with a root meaning of "to send." The Persian term *angaros* means courier, while the word angel derives from the Greek *angelos*, meaning messenger. Angels exist in religious traditions around the world and appear in many forms.

In most traditions, angels are organized in a hierarchy and classified according to the function they perform. As servants of God, they carry out the will of God. They can either aid humans or punish them for disobedient acts. While angels were originally thought to be either benevolent or malevolent, the term angel is generally used today to denote a being possessing the attributes of good. It will be used in that context here.

The Western concept of the angel began in the mythologies of ancient Persia. Zoroastrianism developed a complex hierarchy of angels that influenced Hebrew, Christian, and Islamic theology. Angels also took on characteristics of deities common to Egyptian and Greek folklore. According to Western tradition, angels are incorporeal, spiritual beings who can assume human form at will.

Nowhere is the concept of good more clearly correlated with the aspect of light than in the portrayals of angels. They are associated with the appearance of fire, lightning, and a brilliant light that sometimes envelops their face. This was commonly depicted as the halo in later European art. The idea of the angel as a winged messenger likely stems from the Greek wing-footed god Hermes. In both Old and New Testament canonized texts, angels frequently announced the birth of a prophet or an important figure, including Isaac, Samson, John the Baptist, and Jesus of Nazareth.

It was after the Babylonian captivity and exposure to Zoroastrianism that we see elaborate references to a hierarchy of angelic beings in Jewish literature, including the Biblical Books of Ezekiel and Daniel, the Talmud, Midrashic literature, the Kabbalah, and oral-tradition folklore. The Apocryphal Book of Tobit establishes the healing ministry of angels, and the Pseudepigraphic Book of Enoch presents a detailed angelology.

Chief among the angelic hierarchy were the archangels, or Watchers and Holy Ones. The archangels were seven in number, the same number as the Zoroastrian ahuras. They included Michael and Gabriel, who are mentioned by name in canonized Scripture, Raphael who is mentioned by name in the Book of Tobit and the Book of Enoch, and Uriel, mentioned in the Book of Enoch. In Islam, Gabriel is the angel Jabril who appeared to the prophet Mohammed and revealed to him the wisdom of the Koran.

By the Middle Ages, Christianity had categorized angelic beings into a well-defined hierarchy. The most widely accepted hierarchy was the one devised by Pseudo-Dionysus[14] and later refined by St. Thomas Aquinas as shown in the following table.

Hierarchy	Order	Attribute/Function
First Hierarchy *The Goodness of God*	Seraphim Cherubim Thrones	Fire of Divine Love Divine Knowledge/ Wisdom Divine Justice
Second Hierarchy *Universal Causes*	Dominions Virtues Powers	Divine Regulation Divine Tasks Divine Order
Third Hierarchy *Human Affairs*	Principalities Archangels Angels	Working Order Liaisons/Guardians Messengers

Table 1. The Angelic Hierarchy

As you can see, only the three lower ranks of angelic beings—principalities, archangels, and angels—have a direct relationship with humanity. The other angelic beings are too far removed from the daily affairs of humanity to interact with them on a personal basis.

While considered divine beings in Christian theology, the role of angels remained that of servants and messengers of God, and the worship of angels was strictly forbidden. The modern popular concept of angel has downplayed the angel's role as a stern and impartial authority of God's will and emphasized the aspect of the angel as a guardian spirit whose function is to guide and protect humanity.

Demons as the Embodiment of Evil

While angelic beings personify the characteristics we associate with good, demons represent the aspects of evil. Like angels, the belief in demonic beings is found in cultures throughout the world. In ancient times demons were not specifically evil but were thought of as lesser spirits who were both good and evil according to their inherent nature. It was only with the rise of Christianity, which associated all demons with paganism, that they came to be thought of as purely evil.

The word demon comes from the Greek word *daimon*, which was used by Plato to signify semi-divine beings who served as intermediaries between the Greek gods and humans in much the same way that angels function in Biblical literature. Daimons included beings such as the satyrs as well as the spirits of forests, rivers, and mountains. Sometimes daimons took on the aspect of a ministering spirit who assumed the role of guardian to the living. The philosopher Socrates spoke of his own personal daimon who communicated with him through the "voice within." Socrates' daimon is sometimes equated with the Christian mystic concept of the higher self as reflected in the "still small voice within" (see 1 Kings 19:12 and Psalm 46:10).

Demons were often associated with the spirits of the dead, particularly one's ancestors, such as in the Shinto beliefs of Japan. In some cases these ancestral demons were helpful while in others they brought disease and misfortune. Ceremonies evolved to invoke the help of benevolent demons while other rituals sought to ward off the actions of those that meant harm. The demons commonly portrayed in Tibetan iconography were originally nature spirits associated with a shamanic religion of pre-Buddhist Tibet; they were tamed by the power of the Buddhist saints. We have already addressed the devas or demons common to Zoroastrian beliefs.

In Hindu tradition, demons were associated with the asura or antigods of pre-Vedic India. Tradition says that as the asura grew in number they became jealous of the ahuras and challenged them. A war ensued, the asura were defeated and were relegated to the status of the demons, spirits, and ghosts of India's aboriginal tribes. These demons are thought to produce madness, loss of intellect, and a host of other maladies.

The demonology of Judaism is marked by several systems of classification. The Kabbalah system proposed that all evil emanated from the left pillar of the Tree of Life,[15] and particularly from *Gevurah,* the Judgment of God, where Samael, the fallen angel known as God's poisoner, resided. By the Thirteenth Century, Kabbalahism added ten evil *sephiroth* set in opposition to the ten holy *sephirot* of the Tree of Life. Another system proposed that demons arose from the night terrors, and brought disease, death and unwanted intercourse.

Of particular note among the night demons was Lillith, who according to Jewish folklore was the first wife of Adam. She demanded equality with Adam and failing to get it, left him in anger, cursing the name of God. She was told by three angels to return to Adam but she refused. Her punishment was the loss of the demon children she had spawned with Adam. Since that time Lillith has taken revenge against women in childbirth and newborn infants, whom she seeks to kill during the night hours. She also seeks out men who sleep alone and seduces them so she might produce more demon offspring. Jewish and Christian traditions included the invocation of various amulets as a means of protection against her predations. Lillith probably evolved from Babylonian stories of evil spirits who molested children.

Another spirit found in Jewish folklore is Azazel, who is mentioned by name in the Scriptures. Azazel is identified as a desert spirit who was corrupted through cohabitation with human women. In the Old Testament he is connected with a desert area where the Hebrews performed rites of atonement. Eastern European Jewish culture professed a belief in the *dibbuk*, a demon that takes possession of people and speaks through them, causing them to behave in a demented manner. Elaborate exorcism rites evolved as a means to counter the influence of such spirits.

In Arabic culture, demons, called Jinni, could be good or evil. The Jinni are supernatural beings who can be summoned through the performance of magical rites and compelled into performing a task or service. The Jinni are the origin of the genie popularized by the story of "Aladdin's Lamp" in *Arabian Nights*. Pre-Islamic folklore associated the Jinni with malicious fire spirits of the desert who possessed the ability to shape shift at will. According to Islamic theology the Jinni were created prior to Adam and Eve and were equal in stature to angels. The chief jinn, called Iblis, refused to worship God's son Adam and was cast out of heaven along with his followers. Iblis became equated with the Christian Devil and his followers became equated with demons.

With the rise of Christianity in Europe, the demons of all other cultures were associated with pagan beliefs and took on the connotation of pure evil. By the Fifth Century C.E., the Latin Vulgate used the term daimon to refer to pagan gods in general, as well as to malevolent spirits. During the Middle Ages, demons became associated with witches who were thought to be agents of the Devil. Demons tormented humans in numerous

ways and attacked both males and females through
sexual assault. Deformities were explained away as the
product of human-demon intercourse. Misfortune of
any type, and illnesses of all kinds were directly
attributed to the work of demons.

The Prince of Demons

In the religious beliefs discussed above, there was
usually one demon of extraordinary strength and power.
This demon was credited with leadership of the demonic
hordes, and in some cases, took on aspects of divinity
equal to that of the creator God.

In Hinduism, Vritra, the Adversary of the god Indra,
took on the role of prince of the many ranks of Hindu
demons who plague humans. Buddhist legends depict
demonic figures in monstrous form being led by the
great demon Mara as they unleash their torments upon
humankind. In Zoroastrianism, as we have seen, Angra
Mainyu or Ahriman fulfills the role as the prince of all
demonic evil. Each of these beings personified evil
incarnate within their respective traditions and is
similar to the Christian concept of the Devil, the
Deceiver and Protagonist of the world, the ultimate
incarnation of evil.

4
Historic Concepts of Satan

> ... if the devil does not exist,
> and man has therefore created him,
> he has created him in his own image and likeness.
> Fyodor Dostoyevsky, <u>The Brothers Karamozov</u>

The earliest Biblical references to satan (note the lowercase "s") are secular in nature, and are used to denote an adversary who does not possess any supernatural qualities. Later writings refer to satan as a supernatural being, and describe him as either a "son of God" or as an angel. In these early stories, Satan acts as an agent of God who carries out His will in interactions with humanity. He is subordinate to the will of God and is not an independent force of evil. This is the Satan portrayed in the well-known Biblical story of Job. Centuries later, however, after the Hebrews fell under Persian influence, Satan becomes increasingly identified with evil, and assumes the role of an adversary opposed to God Himself. This is the Satan we see in the temptation of Jesus Christ and in other New Testament writings.

Eventually, Satan would come to be identified with the wicked angels of Hebrew mythology who rebelled against God and were expelled from heaven. The war between the angels of light and the angels of darkness, and the exile of the fallen angels into the realm known as hell would play a crucial part in the development of later Christian theology.

The Secular Origin of "satan"

The word satan comes from the Hebrew word *shaitan* which means adversary, opponent, or accuser. It was a common noun used to describe a secular adversary or enemy. The word was originally used in reference to internal conflict among the Israelites. It later referred to any foreign enemy.

In the First Book of Samuel, Chapter 29, the word satan is used by the Philistine generals in reference to David (the future Israeli king), who at that time wished to ally himself with them in the fight against King Saul. The generals were afraid to permit David's forces to join them in battle, fearing that being a Jew, he would turn against them and become an adversary (satan) to them.

The word is used again in Second Samuel to refer to Abishai, a friend of King David's who repeatedly urged him, much to David's dismay, to put a former ally of Saul's to death. In First Kings, King Solomon remarks that he is glad there are no longer any satans (opponents) to bother him so that he could get on with the building of the Temple. In the Psalms, the secular satan is used as a common noun to denote an accuser, or as a verb meaning to accuse.

Satan as a Supernatural Being

Nowhere in the Bible is the origin of Satan addressed, although he does appear to be a part of the created order. The first reference to "satan" in the Bible portrays the satan as an angel. The Book of Numbers recounts a story in which God sends an angel to act as a satan (obstacle) to impede the journey of Balaam, whose actions have displeased God. The angel blocks Balaam's way and delivers God's message to him. The angel in this story thus acts as an agent or emissary of God who carries out His bidding.

Hebrew mythology of the Sixth Century B.C.E. contains references to satan as a member of the heavenly host. These myths refer to a supernatural satan, one of the *bene* (*ben* meaning son) *ha-elohim* or sons of God, who was sent to hinder human activity.

As the sons of God, the *bene ha-elohim* were thought to be divine beings created by God. Unlike Adam and Eve and their descendants, they had not rebelled against the will of their Creator. These celestial beings were the heavenly host, members of the court of heaven. They are always referred to in the plural and there are inferences that they acted in unison as a group. This makes sense if we consider them as beings who had not rebelled against God and were therefore still joined in the unity of the Creative Force.

Biblical references to satan as a member of the heavenly host include the Second Book of Chronicles, Zechariah, and the Book of Job. In Second Chronicles, God calls together the host of heaven so that they might destroy the evil King Ahab, who allowed the worship of idols. One spirit of the host comes before God and offers to be "a lying spirit in the mouths of his (Ahab's) prophets." God agrees, and tells the spirit to do so, reassuring him that he will succeed. In the Book of Zechariah the prophet tells of a dream in which the high priest Joshua is standing before the "Lord of hosts," along with an angel and Satan (now a capital "S") who is accusing Joshua before God. God rebukes Satan for his efforts, although he appears to remain a member of the heavenly court.

The *bene ha-elohim* appear to be a different order of being than the *ma'lakhim Yahweh*, or angels of God. The sons remained with God, always in His presence, while the angels, as God's messengers and agents, were sent out of the court of heaven to interact with humanity. They were generally depicted in the singular and acted as God's emissaries on specific occasions. Distinctions between the sons of God and the angels of God did blur at times, and there is evidence that on occasion, some of the sons of God interacted with humanity as agents of God in a manner similar to that of angels.

Satan as an Agent of God: The Story of Job

The most well-known example of Satan as an agent of God is found in the Book of Job. Job dates to the Sixth Century B.C.E. and is likely based on a Jewish folktale dating to 1000 B.C.E. Scholars speculate that Job was written by more than one author, with Chapter 28 and Chapters 32-37 being added at a later time. The differences in style and content of these chapters lend credence to this view. The first three chapters tell the original folktale in prose while the remaining chapters tell of the lament of Job in poetic language.

The story opens with a description of the prosperous life of Job, a man that was perfect and right, who feared God and rejected evil. The story then shifts to heaven. "Now there was a day when the sons of God came to present themselves before the Lord, and Satan also came among them." (Job 1:6) God asks Satan what he has been doing and he responds that he has been walking upon the earth. As the conversation continues, God and Satan discuss the merits of Job, with God praising the goodness of Job, and Satan countering that if any evil were to befall him, Job would curse God to His face. At that point God tells Satan "Behold, all that he has is in your power; only upon him do not put forth your hand. So Satan went forth from the presence of the Lord." (Job 1:12) Satan's leaving the presence of God indicates that he was indeed standing in His presence as one of God's sons. A logical question that follows is "can evil stand in the presence of God?" If not, it would then follow that the Satan of Job's story is not evil in himself.

Following this conversation, great misfortune befalls Job. He loses his oxen and sheep, his camels are carried away, his servants are slain, and his sons and daughters lose their lives when a great wind smites his house and kills them. Through all of this tragedy, however, Job remains faithful to God and blesses His name.

In Chapter Two there is another meeting of the heavenly host. "Again there was a day when the sons of God came to present themselves before the Lord, and Satan also came among them to present himself before the Lord." (Job 2:1) Again they speak of Job. This time Satan says that if Job is threatened personally and afflicted in the flesh, he will curse God to His face. God tells Satan, "Behold, he is in your power; only spare his life." (Job 2:6) Satan then afflicts Job with boils from head to foot. In pain and agony he retreats into a pile of ashes. Even Job's wife takes up Satan's cause and urges him to curse God. Job steadfastly refuses.

The chapters that follow are known as "the lament of Job," where he attempts to convince three friends that he has done nothing to deserve this punishment. His lament against this injustice ends in a demand for an answer from God as to why evil has befallen him. In Chapter 38, God answers Job, appearing in the form of a whirlwind, and chastises him in a lengthy speech that says finite human knowledge cannot comprehend the infinite mind of God. What follows are three chapters recounting the glory and majesty of God and His works.

> "Where were you when I laid the foundation of the earth?...when the morning stars sang together, and all the sons of God shouted for joy?" (38:4,7) "Can you bind the chains of the Pleiades or loose the cords of Orion?" (38:31) "Is it at your command that the eagle mounts up and makes his nest on high?" (39:27)

Following God's speech, Job realizes that he has committed the error of pride, and speaks humbly, repenting of his error. "I know that thou canst do all things and that no purpose of thine can be thwarted...I had heard of thee by the hearing of the ear; but now my eye sees thee...." (42:1-5) God then responds that Job has spoken rightly, and blesses him, giving him twice as much as he had before.

The story of Job has been the source of much speculation since it was first set down in writing. It has traditionally been interpreted to be an attempt by the author to address the existence of evil in the world and explain why the innocent suffer. It has been used by Christianity as support for the idea that the human mind cannot comprehend the workings of God and that we should therefore accept God's will without question.

Another interpretation of Job that has been presented is that this story was an attempt to divorce God from evil by making Satan the source of the ills that befell Job. It is true that some scholars have used this story to demonstrate that the evils which plague humanity stem from the actions of Satan, and not God. They point out that while God allows Satan to tempt Job, the evils that befall him originate with Satan. Whether or not this was one of the ideas the author of Job desired to convey, it is true that Job's story has been popularly cited as evidence of Satan's activities on earth.

If we look further, however, we see that in both conversations God sets limits upon how far Satan can go in his actions against Job. The fact that Satan accepts God's instructions without question and does not argue against them indicates that he accepts a role subservient to God. Most scholars accept that God permits the testing of Job, and that Satan could not have taken any action without God's permission and authority. In this respect the Satan who visits evil upon the righteous Job is acting as an agent of God who is carrying out His will. This is supported by the fact that Job himself attributes his misfortune to God rather than to Satan and that God acknowledges this fact in His response to Job.

The role Satan plays in this story is very interesting, for it shows characteristics of both submission and independence. As noted above, Satan's acceptance of the limits God sets implies that Satan is subservient. Yet during the first meeting between God and Satan, God asks Satan where he has been, implying that He, the omnipotent Creator, did not know Satan's whereabouts. During the course of their conversation, Satan **argues** with God and presents a dissenting opinion concerning the righteousness of Job. He then **challenges** God to allow a testing of Job, and God accepts his challenge! This certainly seems to give Satan the appearance of independent thought and action.

While the story of Job was most likely an attempt to address the question of the existence of evil in the world and explain why it is sometimes visited upon innocent people, it also sows the seeds, intentionally or unintentionally, of the idea of Satan as a purveyor of evil, an independent being who argues and contends with God as an adversary, rather than an agent of His will. This Satan-type closely parallels the evil Ahriman "satan" of Zoroastrian belief that would develop more fully in the pseudepigraphic writings of later Judaism and fully culminate in the Satan of Christian theology.

Satan as an Adversary to God

The idea of Satan as an independent adversary opposed to God was first voiced in Jewish writings that date to the Babylonian exile when the Israelites came under the Persian influence of Zoroastrianism.   The First Book of Chronicles is a retelling of Judean history, written in the Fourth Century B.C.E. In Chapter 21 there is a reference to a Satan who convinces King David to conduct a census of his people in direct defiance of God's wishes. This Satan is not portrayed as a son of God nor as an angel of God; he is simply God's adversary who seeks to tempt God's servant.

It is interesting that this very same census story was recounted several centuries earlier in the Book of Second Samuel. Yet in Samuel, it is the Lord who tempts David to take a census "And again the anger of the Lord was kindled against Israel, and he incited David against them saying, 'Go, number Israel and Judah.'" (2 Samuel 24:1)

What happened in the intervening centuries between Second Samuel and First Chronicles is that the Israelites became acquainted with the dualistic beliefs of Zoroastrianism that saw good and evil as independent and opposing forces. Under this influence, the God of the Old Testament increasingly lost any aspects of wrath and judgment while Satan grew in stature as a force of evil. The author of Chronicles cannot comprehend that an all-good God would tempt man and therefore attributes this act to His adversary, Satan.

It was also at this time that Satan came to be identified as one of the fallen angels who rebelled against God and were expelled from heaven. Other fallen angels included Beelzebub, Azazel, and Belial, all of whom were portrayed as increasingly evil beings. Satan began to take on an increasingly prominent evil personality of independent stature and was eventually credited with leadership of this group. From there it was a short step to seeing Satan as the supreme antagonist opposed to God, the embodiment of all evil.

Changing Concepts of Satan in the Pseudepigraphia

The Pseudepigraphia is a collection of ancient Jewish writings composed during a several hundred-year period between 250 B.C.E. to 200 C.E. Some of the pseudepigraphic books were later expanded or rewritten by Christians. They serve as a bridge between the ideas found in the Old and New Testaments. They were erroneously attributed to some of the major Old Testament figures including Abraham, Moses, David, and Solomon, hence the name "pseude" (false). Many of these writings are apocalyptic in nature and focus on the origin, purpose, and final resolution of evil. They appear to have been heavily influenced by the Zoroastrian dualistic concept of good and evil. Some prominent pseudepigraphic books include the Book of Enoch, the Secrets of Enoch, the Books of Adam and Eve, the Book of Jubilees, the Testament of the Twelve Patriarchs, and the Books of Maccabees.

A review of the Pseudepigraphia shows the gradual development of Satan from an adversarial being, similar to that described in Chronicles, to an independent power of absolute evil. As this concept develops in various books, we see Satan referred to by different names, including Mastema, Azazel, Semjaza, and Satanail.

The Book of Jubilees contains a retelling of the testing of Abraham found in Chapter 22 of Genesis, where God instructs Abraham to sacrifice his son Isaac as a demonstration of his faith and obedience. Abraham follows God's instructions and is about to take his son's life when God speaks to him and stays his hand saying "...for now I know that you fear God, seeing you have not withheld your son, your only son, from me." (Genesis 22:12) In the Book of Jubilees, however, it is not God who tempts Abraham but Mastema, a Satan-figure. As the story unfolds it is Mastema who convinces God to test Abraham in much the same way that Satan argued with God for the testing of Job.

In another segment of Jubilees, Mastema again appears when God is about to banish all evil spirits, reputed to be the unnatural offspring of angels and human women, from earth. Mastema, addressed as the "chief of the spirits," asks God to allow some of the evil spirits to remain on earth so that he might accomplish his appointed work, namely the continued temptation of humanity. God agrees, and allows one-tenth of the portion of evil spirits to remain under Mastema's direction. The idea of an army of satanic beings led by Satan carried over into later Christian writings. What is often neglected, however, is the idea that the Mastema-Satan character has a role to play in the moral development of humanity.

The Book of Enoch tells the story of two celestial beings, Azazel and Semjaza, who are identified as being among the "Watchers" who never sleep (guardian angels). This is the same Azazel who, centuries earlier, was mentioned in the Book of Leviticus as an evil demon of the desert. Together they incite a host of angels to lust after human women and to descend to earth and take them as wives. They taught women the ways of seduction and taught men the art of warfare. The offspring of this unnatural union were hideous monsters who fought among themselves and brought devastation to the earth. God then orders four of the archangels, Michael, Gabriel, Raphael, and Uriel, to intervene and destroy the monstrous evil spirits and imprison the Watchers until the final judgment. Uriel is sent to warn Noah of the coming flood that will cleanse the earth and destroy any remaining remnants of evil.

Much of the symbolism used in the Book of Enoch made its way into later Christian writings. Of particular note are references to the rebellious angels as "fallen stars" who burn as they fall to earth. Also of note is the "abyss of fire," the place into which the Watchers will be cast following their judgment at the end of time. The abyss of fire also appears in the Apocalypse of Abraham when Abraham tells Azazel to become the "burning coal of the furnace of the earth." The Christian concept of Satan as the leader of fallen angels who rules over the domain of hell until the final Day of Judgment no doubt traces its origin to these earlier writings.

In the Book of Adam and Eve, the fall of Satan and the other angels is attributed not to their desire for human women, but by their refusal to bow down before God's new creations—Adam and Eve. The archangel Michael immediately obeyed God's edict, but Satan refused, saying that he had been created first and they should therefore bow to him. Michael points out that these beings were created by God in His own image and are therefore deserving of this show of respect. This response only angers Satan and he replies that he will set his seat above the stars of heaven and become like God himself. The desire to make himself equal with God is *hubris*, the sin of pride, and for this Satan and those who followed his example are punished by being cast from heaven and thrown down upon the earth.

The idea of Satan being jealous of God's new creations is carried on in the Islamic story of Iblis, the angel who fell because of his hatred and jealousy of the first humans created by God. The Book of Adam and Eve also identifies the serpent in the Garden of Eden as an agent of Satan, through whom he tempted and deceived the newly created couple.

The fall of the angels being the result of sinful pride is also found in the Secrets of Enoch. In this story Enoch visits the seven levels of heaven where, on the second level, he sees angels being held in darkness until the day of final judgment. Enoch discovers that the prince of these angels, Satanail, is being held in the fifth heaven, along with an order of angels called Grigori, from whose ranks Satanail and the rebelling angels had originated. The sad Grigori, who mourn the fall of their comrades, tell Enoch how Satanail had an impossible thought that he might set his throne above the clouds and become equal in stature to God. As punishment for this affront of pride against God, Satanail and his followers were exiled from God's presence.

By the First Century B.C.E., the portrait of Satan

given in the Pseudepigraphia had evolved into that of an independent being of pure evil, similar to the popular concept of Satan held by many people today. In the Testament of the Twelve Patriarchs, Satan is called Beliar, and is depicted by the twelve sons of Jacob (the twelve patriarchs) as "the prince of deceit" whose "works oppose the law of the Lord. He rules over all souls that are inclined to evil; and is pleased when people...serve not God, but their own lusts."[16] The patriarchs go on to say that in the latter days the wicked will cling to Beliar but that the Lord will ultimately redeem those seduced by him through the work of a savior who will put an end to sin.

The portrait of Satan depicted in the Pseudepigraphia thus shows a progressive development from a being who was first pictured as an adversary or accuser of Abraham, to an agent of God who is active in humanity's development, and later as a fallen angel who was cast from heaven due to sinful and erroneous thought. It culminates in the form of Beliar, a prince of deceit who stands in opposition to the way of God and seeks to lead all souls into the darkness of sin and perversity. It is evident that many of the concepts and stories contained in the Pseudepigraphia have their origin in Zoroastrian beliefs and legends. It is also clear that many of these ideas were adopted by early Christian writers and had a definite impact on the Christian concept of Satan.

The New Testament Satan: Mighty Enemy of God and Man

By the time the writers of the New Testament were telling the story of Jesus of Nazareth, the concept of Satan was well defined. Satan was perceived as an angel of high order who was cast away from God's presence due to his own wicked desires and pride. He became

the master of other fallen angels and a host of evil
spirits. He serves as the evil prince of the world,
tempting all those he can seduce to turn from the ways
of the Lord. He will, however, eventually be defeated by
the forces of good led by the Savior, and thrown into the
great abyss or hell.

He appears in the Gospels of Matthew, Mark, Luke,
and John, the Book of Acts, Hebrews, Jude, First Peter,
and many of the letters of Paul. Satan also appears in
the Book of Revelation. In addition to being called
Satan, he is referred to as "the Devil" who subjects Jesus
to a series of three temptations in the wilderness
(Matthew 4), "the Wicked One" (Matthew 13 and Mark
4), "Father of Lies" (John 8), "Ruler of Demons"
(Matthew 9), "Lord of Death" (Hebrews 2), and "the
Great Dragon" (Revelation 12).

While New Testament writings detail Satan's
activities, they do not address his origin other than to
make reference to the fact that he is an angel who fell
from heaven. Further, there is no analysis of Satan's
characteristics or metaphysical dimensions. This is
likely due to the fact that by this time the Christian
community presupposed the concept of Satan.

A good example of this can be seen in the incident in
which the enemies of Jesus attribute his ability to
exorcise demons to the power of Beelzebub, the prince
of demons. Jesus answers that a servant of Satan would
not cast out demons because that would weaken the
demonic house against itself. Note that Jesus does not
question the existence of a prince of demons but rather
identifies Beelzebub with Satan. Jesus' response and its
unquestioned acceptance indicate that the belief in
Satan as a prince of demons was well established in
Jesus' day. It should be noted that the idea of Satan as a
prince of an army of demons, be they fallen angels or
evil spirits, is not found in any Old Testament writings,
but is well-documented in the Pseudepigraphia.

The Temptation of Christ

Satan's role in the temptation of Christ, as told in the Gospels of Matthew and Luke, is a well-known Biblical story. At the start of Jesus' ministry, which began with His baptism by John in the River Jordan, Jesus retreats to the wilderness so he may be "tempted by the devil." He had fasted for forty days and nights when the devil appeared to him and said, "If you are the Son of God, command these stones to become loaves of bread." (Matthew 4:3) Jesus refuses saying, "Man shall not live by bread alone, but by every word that proceeds from the mouth of God." (4:4) The devil then takes Jesus to the holy city, sets him on the top of the temple and bids him "If you are the Son of God, throw yourself down, for it is written, He will give his angels charge of you and on their hands they will bear you up...." (4:6) Jesus refuses the second temptation by saying "Again it is written, you shall not tempt the Lord your God." (4:7) Next the devil takes Jesus to a mountaintop and shows him all the kingdoms and glory of the world and says "All these I will give you, if you will fall down and worship me." (4:9) Jesus refuses this final temptation by saying "Begone, Satan! for it is written, 'You shall worship the Lord your God and him only shall you serve." (9:10) Following this rebuke, the devil leaves and the angels of God appear and come to minister to Jesus' needs.

This story contains within it the most compelling example of the means Satan most commonly uses in his role as tempter. First, he preys upon a person while in a weakened state, in this case, a weakened physical state caused by forty days of fasting. He starts by offering a small thing of little consequence in an effort to reassure that acceptance of this one small thing will be all right. For Jesus this turned out be the simple necessity of food. Satan will also resort to using God's own words against Him in an attempt lure the person away from the truth. By using God's words of truth in a perverted way he seeks to trick the person into believing that his deceit is right and just. Finally, Satan tempts the person with an offer that he thinks cannot be refused, an offer usually based on worldly power and might. A point which needs to be noted here is that Satan's ability to act as tempter only extends as far as a person is willing to allow it to go. As soon as Jesus tells Satan to leave him, he does.

The story of the temptation of Christ thus serves as a model of the way in which Satan tempts humankind. From this idea it was a short step to conceive of Satan not only as an enemy of God, but as the personal enemy of all humanity.

Satan as a Personal Enemy

Examples of Satan as the tempter and seducer of human beings everywhere are well documented in the New Testament. Not only is there a description of his temptation of Christ, but the Gospels of John and Luke also attest that he was responsible for the corruption of Judas and for Simon Peter's denial of knowing Jesus. In the Book of Acts, Peter suggests that Satan not only lies, but also puts lies in the hearts of others.

In the letters of St. Paul we find many references to the way in which Satan interferes with human activities on a continual basis. He recounts Satan's role in bringing sin and evil into the world. He counsels the members of a church to settle their differences so that Satan might not have an advantage over them. He comments that Satan is near at hand and will seek every opportunity to cause a person to lose self-control and have lustful thoughts. He notes that it is the devil who put lies into a person's heart. He considers Satan as the cause of all pain and suffering, noting that an angel of

Satan caused his own physical affliction. He blames Satan for the events that hinder his and Timothy's return to the church of Thessalonia.

In New Testament writings, therefore, Satan moves beyond being an adversary who contends with God and becomes a very personal devil who stands at our side, ever ready to seduce and tempt us. The followers of Christ are urged to be on guard at all times lest Satan gain the upper hand. "Be sober, be watchful. Your adversary the devil, prowls around like a roaring lion, seeking some one to devour." (I Peter 5:8)

Satan as Ruler of the World

New Testament writers also considered Satan as the ruler of this world. Remember that the Pseudepigraphia states that Satan was given dominion over the earth when he was exiled from heaven. Jesus himself affirms this idea when he tells Pontius Pilate "My kingship is not of this world...." (John 18:36) This comment has been interpreted to mean that Jesus came to establish a spiritual kingdom rather than a kingdom of earthly power and might.

Some references indicate that Satan is not the direct ruler of this world but is the power behind the ruler. This concept is most evident in the Book of Revelation where Satan, as the Great Dragon, gives his power to a "beast" that comes out of the sea and to a "false prophet" sometimes called the "antichrist." The beast and the antichrist are two of the most popular conceptions of Satan.

The description of Satan given in Revelation is a complete characterization of all the traits and attributes that had previously been credited to him by various sources. Satan is adversary to God, fallen angel, prince of demons, tempter and seducer of humanity, lord of hell, ruler of this world, purveyor of evil, and the source of all human ills and suffering. The secular "satan" had become Satan the Diabolical, the mighty antagonist of God and humanity, the Devil of Christian theology.

Satan as The Christian Devil

While the major characteristics of Satan were established in the writings of the New Testament, certain aspects of his character and his relationship to evil were still subject to speculation by later Christian scholars. The works of three well-known theologians, Origen, St. Augustine, and John Calvin, represent three major viewpoints on this subject.

Origen: Satan as Lucifer,
the Fallen Star of Morning

Origen, 185-254 C.E., was a great theologian and scholar of the early Christian Church. He attempted to synthesize Christian Scripture with Greek philosophy, especially Neoplatonism and Stoicism. Although many of his writings have disappeared, his literary output was tremendous. He composed a critical text of the Old Testament, wrote commentaries on Matthew and John, authored a dogmatic treatise on God and the world, and completed a refutation of paganism.

His writings also serve as some of the best examples of Christian mysticism. He believed that the highest good was to become like God, not through the intercession of the Holy Mother, saints, or priests, but through progressive enlightenment on an individual level. Some of his ideas, including a belief in reincarnation, were controversial and fell out of favor long after his death. His writings were condemned as heretical at the Council of Constantinople in 553 C.E. Nevertheless, his influence on early Christian theology remained, and he is considered the most influential theologian of the church prior to St. Augustine. Many of his ideas are being reexamined by Christian theologians today.

Origen identified Satan with Lucifer, the bright morning star, spoken of by the prophet Isaiah.

> "How art thou fallen from heaven, O Lucifer, son of the morning!...For thou has said in thine heart, I will ascend into heaven, I will exalt my throne above the stars of God...I will ascend above the heights of the clouds; I will be like the most High. Yet thou shalt be brought down to hell, to the sides of the pit." (Isaiah 14:12-14 KJV)

While other theologians believed this was a reference to a Babylonian king of Isaiah's time, Origen maintained that it was a reference to Satan. His interpretation was based on a comparison of Isaiah with a text from the Gospel of Luke in which Jesus used a similar analogy when he said, "I saw Satan fall like lightning from heaven." (Luke 10:18) Based on a comparison of these two texts, Origen concluded that Satan was Lucifer, the name that described the brightness of the angel before he was cast from heaven.

Evil, according to Origen, was the result of Satan's impossible thought that he could be equal with God. Adam and Even then repeated this sin of pride by defying God in the Garden of Eden. Origen also proposed a powerful salvation theory, in which the infinite love and mercy of God extends to all his creations, including Satan and the fallen angels. The idea of the ultimate redemption of all creations is also found in Zoroastrianism. This theory, however, was later rejected by the Christian Church.

St. Augustine: The Moral Evil of Satan

In addressing the question of evil in the world, St. Augustine distinguished between natural and moral evil, and echoed some of the ideas found in the Book of Job. Natural evil, such as a flood, was not really evil from God's point of view. Humans perceive it as evil because we cannot comprehend the whole picture.

The only true evil, moral evil, was the willful deprivation of good which occurred when beings willfully distorted their true God-given natures. The entrance of this type of evil into the world occurred when Adam and Eve ate the forbidden fruit of the Tree of Knowledge so that they might become as God was. According to St. Augustine, evil was unavoidable because of humankind's sinful nature. When St. Augustine linked evil with original sin and sinful behavior, he permanently tied evil to issues of morality.

The difference between human moral sin and Satan's sin of pride was that Adam and Eve were tempted to this behavior; the thought did not originate with them. Because of this, they and their descendants could be restored to their original state of grace through God's mercy. Satan's desire to reject his nature as an angel and be as God came from his own mind. Since this thought originated in his own mind, Satan had condemned himself forever. The idea of an eternally damned Satan became a main doctrine of Christianity.

John Calvin: Satan as a Creation of God

The French theologian John Calvin, 1509-1564 C.E., was one of the leading proponents of the Protestant Reformation. Schooled in humanism, the classics and theology, he experienced a Protestant conversion during the years 1526-1531 C.E. He thereafter devoted his life to the Reformation effort, writing a number of influential commentaries on the books of the Bible. He also was responsible for the establishment of a lay movement within the Presbyterian Church that had a great impact throughout Europe.

Calvin's writings confirmed much that had already been written in Catholic theology regarding Satan. He described Satan as self-corrupted, malicious in nature, the cause of everything evil, and the ruler of this world.

Yet Calvin was careful to emphasize that Satan was not an independent being, but a creation of God and therefore subject to His will. In fact, he states that Satan cannot do anything contrary to the will and consent of God. He further points out that while Satan tempts us, he never masters us. He tends to see the elaborate descriptions of Satan's power as a warning sign or reminder so that we might be more cautious and vigilant in our struggle against the sin of pride.

The idea of Satan as a creation of God subject to his will is reminiscent of the earlier concept of Satan as an agent of God. The natural question that follows would be "if Satan cannot defy God, are his actions therefore in accordance with God's will and desires?" Unfortunately, Calvin did not address this issue further in his writings.

Modern Developments

While Christian theologians may have disagreed on some of the aspects of Satan's nature, the Christian concept of the Devil as a fallen angel who brought evil and suffering to humanity was well established in Western culture. In many cases, the popular or folk concept of Satan was more terrifying than that portrayed in Christian doctrine. The majority of the people believed the Devil to be an all-powerful demonic being who tempted and attacked them at every turn, and against whose assaults they could do little.

The art and literature of the medieval and Renaissance eras helped further this picture. Artists portrayed the Devil as a monstrous being with horns, hooves and a tail, folklore described demonic attacks on people as they slept, and people feared they would be cursed for eternity in Dante's *Inferno* for their sins. In *Paradise Lost*, John Milton dramatized the story of Satan and his demonic legions so all posterity might know the diabolical power of the Devil. This concept of Satan persisted for hundreds of years. Even today the mention of "the Devil" still brings to mind the same vivid images.

As you can see, the concept of Satan has changed dramatically over the course of human history. The myths and legends surrounding this being grew to such a proportion that we began to think of Satan as an equal to God, with powers rivaling those of God Himself. When considering who and what Satan may be, we need to remember that our perception of Satan has indeed changed from the original concept of Satan as a secular enemy.

We also need to remember that neither Satan nor any other forces of evil have any power over us if we reject them. Jesus demonstrated this very clearly when he told Satan to depart and Satan did. We need to understand that the only power evil has over us is the power we give it. When we realize this, we cease to see Satan as an all-powerful supernatural being capable of shaking the very foundations of heaven itself. Rather, we see the Satan story as a reflection of the continuing battle between good and evil. We come to understand that Satan may simply be a hidden aspect of the dark side of ourselves.

5
Secular Thought

The question "Am I my brother's keeper" could only be asked in a society in which men had ceased to be involved with one another. It could never have been asked in the earlier stages of man's social development. Man had to be his brother's keeper; or else there would have been no men left to tell the tale.
Ashley Montagu, <u>The Human Revolution</u>

The philosophies and religious systems of thought discussed in the previous chapters all saw good and evil as manifestations of the divine, whether it be as cosmic forces or in the form of individual divine beings. Science, however, does not concern itself with the existence of the divine. It is concerned solely with the study and measurement of observable phenomena.

With the advent of the scientific revolution, the universe was no longer thought of as a living organism, mysterious and indecipherable. The works of Copernicus, Galileo, Newton, and Descartes showed that the universe was not a mysterious, living organism but a precise machine, devoid of intelligence, and subject to the laws of mathematics and physics. Scientists believed that the universe could be analyzed through intellectual reasoning. Man, a divine creation of God and highest order of the old universe was reduced to the level of a rational animal as scientists began to question the existence of the soul itself. The distinction between body and soul, common to so many religions, became a distinction between mind and body, while good and evil became a matter of human nature.

The Duality of Human Nature

Human nature[17] is defined as the fundamental characteristics, qualities, and disposition shared by all members of the human species. It also includes human behavior, which is the standard range of conduct typical of the human species. It refers to the motivating factors that control and influence behavior. The fact that we see both good and evil in human behavior led to the conclusion that human beings must possess a dual nature, caused by two opposing forces which are in constant conflict with one another. While theologians believed that this duality was a direct reflection of the conflict between the soul and the flesh, secular thinkers, who questioned the very existence of the soul itself, saw this as a distinction between the mind and the body.

The body-mind duality reached its zenith during the Seventeenth Century through the writings of the French philosopher Rene Descartes, who declared that the body and mind were two separate and distinct substances. Descartes believed that human nature was determined by innate ideas implanted in the mind by God. These innate ideas, which included the divine, the soul, morality, and other abstract theorems, could be understood through reason. For Descartes, the highest expression of good was found in the application of human reason.

Another school of thought, represented by Thomas Hobbes, an English philosopher of the Seventeenth Century, held that the natural state of humanity is "nasty, brutish, and short," implying that human nature is evil. Hobbes believed that it was only through society that humanity achieved peace and security.

A third view was championed by another English philosopher and political theorist, John Locke. Locke argued that at birth, the mind is a *tabula rosa* or blank slate, which is shaped by experience. A person's environment thus has the most influence upon his development. Locke believed that humanity was neither inherently good nor evil, but advocated that experience determines what behaviors a person will manifest.

In the true tradition of the Enlightenment, Sigmund Freud, the father of psychology, sought to bring human consciousness under the scrutiny of rational investigation. Ironically, it was his psychoanalytic studies that had the effect of undermining the rationalism of human thought. As Freud probed the depths of the human psyche, he explored the meaning of dreams and fantasy, discovered the Oedipus complex, exposed infantile sexuality, revealed the psychological relevance of mythology, and laid bare the mechanisms of resistance, repression, and projection. He concluded that all human behavior stemmed from two primary instinctual drives: sexual pleasure and aggression.

Suddenly the mind was no longer the seat of rational thought and analysis, but a seething cauldron of irrational forces, amoral, aggressive, erotic, and perverse. Not only was man's divinity called into question, but his very humanity as well.[18] The carnal influences, the seat of evil, once thought to be the domain of the body, were shown to exist in the recesses of the human mind.

The Nature Versus Nurture Debate

In the Twentieth Century, the body-mind dichotomy expressed itself as the nature versus nurture debate, as modern scientists sought to determine how much of human behavior was caused by genetic factors and how much was a result of environment or learning. The scientific community was divided into two major camps. Biological scientists claimed that human behavior was determined by innate instincts—heredity. The innate aggressionists believed that evil, as demonstrated by violence and aggression, was an inherent part of human nature. Social scientists on the other hand, claimed that human behavior was determined by learning and culture—environment. This meant that evil was a learned behavior and not an inherited part of human nature.

The violent nature of the 1960s spawned intense public interest in the subject of human aggression. The views of the innate aggressionists were based on the work of Konrad Lorenz, a Nobel Prize winner in physiology and medicine. In 1966, Lorenz published *On Aggression,* wherein he used his zoological studies to support his view that aggression is an instinctual human behavior.   Basing most of his conclusions on data derived from observations of animal behavior, Lorenz concluded that humans have an innate instinct for aggression that was spontaneous in nature and aided in the survival of the species. He further proposed that the rapid growth of culture and its social inhibitions prevented the natural expression of aggression, which was then redirected in terms of violent behavior enacted upon others.

These ideas gained a popular following through the publication of *African Genesis* and *The Territorial Imperative* by Robert Ardrey, *Human Aggression* by Anthony Storr and The *Naked Ape* by Desmond Morris. Ardrey was a dramatist who turned to the writing of ethological and anthropological material. He claimed that humans are territorial predators whose natural instinct is to kill with a weapon.   Storr's writings combined the instinct theory with psychoanalysis; much of his work was based on psychopathological case studies. Morris concluded that while he could find no evidence of the existence of an innate and spontaneous aggressive drive, aggression is a genetically governed response to environmental stimuli.   These works contained the same basic thesis that human aggressive behavior, as manifested in war, crime, and personal and destructive sadistic behavior, is due to a genetically programmed instinct that needs to be released at spontaneous intervals.[19]

The views of the innate aggressionists were promptly challenged by social scientists who refuted their theories, faulting the methodologies used in the studies. They criticized the excessive use of animal analogy in place of hard data, anthropomorphizing (giving animals human characteristics), the exclusion of contrary evidence, and neglect of the role of learning in human behavior.

A number of field studies on the behavior of humankind's closest relatives, the great apes, revealed little of the typical, aggressive, brutish behavior of popular folklore. Orangutans were shown to be solitary primates with no overt violent tendencies. The myth of King Kong was debunked by the work of Diane Fossey who showed that gorillas were really gentle giants, vegetarians who would withdraw rather than fight in threatening situations.[20] Millions of people throughout the world are familiar with the intelligent and heart-warming ways of the Gombe chimpanzees made famous through Jane Goodall's fieldwork.[21] In view of these studies, the idea of humans born of a violent and savage past where brute strength was king just did not seem to make sense. If modern day apes lacked significant aggressive behavior patterns, how could we suppose that our common ancestors possessed them?

It was the work of anthropologist Ashley Montagu, however, which served as the main counterpoint to such ideas. *Man and Aggression*, edited by Montagu, was a collection of essays by various social scientists that pointed out the flaws in the methodology of the innate aggressionists. In *The Human Revolution*, Montagu makes the case that in early human evolution, the highest selective value was upon intelligence while preconditioned behavior such as instinct became less important. As a small, unspecialized species possessing little natural strength or defensive traits, early humans survived through cooperation, which ensured their survival against the elements and other predatory species. As a physically weak species with no natural defenses, early humans needed one another to survive. Killing even one member of the group could have a disastrous effect upon the chances of survival for everyone.

In other works Montagu drew upon fossil evidence, prehistory, and histories of early civilizations to demonstrate that violent, aggressive behavior developed along with the rise of civilization. He made a correlation between increasing aggression and problems such as overpopulation, stratification, and the uneven distribution of wealth. He also cited ethnological studies of many nonliterate societies that lack any aggressive or violent tendencies. Montagu concludes,

> "The fact is that as man has advanced in civilization he has become increasingly, not less, violent and warlike. The violence that has been attributed to his original nature has, in fact been acquired predominately within the relatively recent period of man's cultural evolution."[22]

Today's scientific mainstream accepts the view that human behavior, good and evil, is a result of our biological heritage, cultural conditioning, and environmental upbringing. Humans are born with the capacity for aggressive behavior just as they are born with the capacity for nonviolence and love. The presence or absence of such behavior depends upon a combination of hereditary factors and culture. Humans are neither inherently good nor evil, but possess the capacity for both.

Part Two
A Metaphysical View

It is clear that the Edgar Cayce readings support a metaphysical philosophy that addresses the who, the how, and the why of human existence. Many readings were given in answer to questions concerning who we really are, how we came into being, and why we were created. In order to understand Cayce's view of good and evil, we need to first understand the essential principles that stand as the cornerstones of his philosophy. The readings are, of course, subject to the interpretation of the reviewer. While others may come up with different variations, I believe that any student of the Cayce readings would agree that the following five points can be considered as primary principles of Cayce's metaphysical system. Each primary principle, along with several key ideas, is presented below.

∗ **All existence is an expression of the one Creative Force.**
➤ There is only one force, power, or spirit in the universe.
➤ The Creative Force is Absolute Being, omniscient and omnipresent.
➤ The Creative Force is responsible for bringing all existence into being.
➤ The Creative Force can be thought of as the God-Force, Spirit, God, Divine Will, and Universal Mind.

∗ **All existence is governed by Universal Laws.**
➤ The Universal Laws are unbreakable, unchangeable principles that operate in all phases of life and existence.
➤ The Universal Laws operate for all beings, everywhere, all the time, whether one is aware of them or not.
➤ The Universal Laws operate on the spiritual, mental, and physical planes.
➤ The Universal Laws are the keys to the operation of life, your relationship with the Universe, and your relationships with others.

∗ **All existence occurs first in spirit, then in mind, and then in physical manifestation.**
➤ Spirit is the First Cause, the life force or unlimited creative energy within us.
➤ Mind is an active force, an essence that flows between Spirit and the material plane.
➤ All manifestations of life, in any plane of consciousness, are crystallizations of spirit and thought.

- ➢ The macrocosm, or outer universe, is reflected in the microcosm, or inner self.
- * **All human beings are spiritual beings, endowed with creative abilities and freedom of will.**
  - ➢ The soul was created when God, as Spirit, extended itself and brought individualized expressions of itself into being.
  - ➢ We were created to be co-creators and companions with the God-Force.
  - ➢ To be truly "as God," the soul was given free will so that it might choose for itself.
  - ➢ Through the will, we can create in accordance with spiritual ideals and create goodness and order, or we can defy Divine Will and create chaos and destruction.
- * **All life has purpose and meaning.**
  - ➢ We have chosen to come to "earth school" and learn certain lessons, through the Universal Laws, so that we might return to our original state of unity with the Creative Force.
  - ➢ Life is synchronistic; each experience we encounter, every person we met, and each relationship we engage in, happens for a reason.
  - ➢ We are responsible for our thoughts and our actions, and will inevitably face the consequences of our choices.
  - ➢ Life is the experience of our choices.

6
The Universal Forces

...man was made a little lower than the angels,
yet with that power to become one with God,
while the angel remains the angel.
Edgar Cayce Reading 900-16

All Force is One Force

The Edgar Cayce readings, like many of the traditional belief systems we have discussed, see the divine as both abstract and personal. In Reading 1158-14, Cayce was asked:

> "Is it correct when praying to think of God as impersonal force or energy, everywhere present; or as an intelligent listening mind, which is aware of every individual on earth and who intimately knows everyone's needs and how to meet them?"

The answer given was:

> "Both! For He is also the energies in the finite moving in material manifestation. He is also the Infinite, with the awareness. And thus as ye attune thy own consciousness, thy own awareness, the unfoldment of the presence within beareth witness with the presence without."

When speaking of the divine in the abstract, the readings use the several terms, including Creative Force, God-Force, and Spirit. These all convey the same meaning and can be used interchangeably.

The readings present a monistic perspective and repeatedly state that all force is one force. The concept of monism[23] is one of the strongest themes found in the readings, as demonstrated in the following excerpts.

> "All force is as one force. Hence the universal forces. All knowledge is as one knowledge." (254-30)

> "ONE is the beginning, to be sure. Before ONE is nothing. After ONE is nothing, if all be IN ONE - as ONE God, ONE Son, ONE Spirit. This, then, the ESSENCE of ALL force, ALL manners of energies. All activities EMANATE from the ONE." (5751-1)

> "ALL force, all power that is manifested in the earth, EMANATES from a spiritual or God-force..." (815-3)

> "For, life is the manifestation of that force ye call God, in whatever form it may appear; and is ONE!" (2505-1)

> "In the manifestation of all power, force, motion, vibration, that which impels, that which detracts, is in its essence of one force, one source..." (262-52)

If all force, all energy, all life is one, it would follow that both good and evil originate from the Creative Force. According to the readings, however, this is not the case. Good is an aspect of the original creation. It is the original state of the soul when it recognizes its oneness with the Creative Force and acts in accordance with the divine ordering of the universe.

Evil, on the other hand, was brought into existence through the **activities of the soul**, and not by the hand of God. Reading 262-52, quoted above, continues: "As to what has been done or accomplished by or through the activity of entities that have been delegated powers in activity is another story."

According to the readings, good and evil are different manifestations of the same force. Good is the expression of creative ability in accordance with Divine Will and Universal Law. Evil is the expression of creative ability in ways that are contrary to Divine Will. While the result we create is different, the energy or force is the same. It is how we apply that force that determines whether we create good or whether we create evil.

> "Ideas may be merely thoughts. As they run the course through those activities and minds of individuals, they may become crimes or they become miracles, dependent upon that with which the individual entity gives the thought or the idea to an ideal..." (5250-1)

This idea is very similar to that of the mana beliefs discussed earlier. Mana, or the creative energy force, is neutral. It is the intention of the person harnessing and directing that force which determines whether the created result is good or evil. It parallels the beliefs of Taoism and Stoicism that despite appearances, all opposites are really one and the same. It also contains some of the elements found in Plato's dualistic philosophy, particularly the idea that evil is not an original creation.

The abstract, omnipotent, and omniscient Creative Force noted in the readings is also portrayed as a very personal God. As Reading 391-4 tells us,

"KNOW that the Creative Energy called God may be *as personal as an individual will allow* [italics for author's emphasis] same to be; for the Spirit is in the image of the Creative Forces and seeks manifestation. It may take that personality, that will be allowed by the individual itself..."

Many of the personal references to God in the readings parallel Judaic-Christian teachings. God is portrayed as the living God who walks and talks with those who seek to follow His ways, "So, walk and talk oft with Him...For He hath promised to meet thee, in humbleness, in love, in patience, in kindness." (5030-1) He is a God of wrath only to those who chose self over Divine Will, "only a God of wrath to those who defy and say 'I – yea I – will do this or that.' For of thyself ye can do nothing, only as He in His love and mercy may show thee the way." (3660-1).

Despite our many failings, He is also a God of love and mercy, "Through the periods of thy sojourns in the earth, ye have oft defied the living God, and yet He hath loved thee and hath again given thee an opportunity, here, now, today, if ye hear His voice." (3660-1)

Similarly, evil is also seen as being both abstract and personal. Reading 262-52 states,

"Hence that force which rebelled in the unseen forces (or in spirit) that came into activity, was that influence which has been called Satan, the Devil, the Serpent; they are One. That of REBELLION! Hence, when man in any activity rebels against the influences of good he harkens to the influence of evil rather than the influence of good...Evil is rebellion...As there is, then, a personal savior, there is the personal devil."

Evil therefore is viewed in abstract terms as the spirit of rebellion and also personalized in the being known as Satan. In other readings, Satan is referred to as the Dragon, the Lord of Darkness, and the Lord of Rebellion.

The readings advise us, however, that we should not take these personalized expressions of good and evil to mean that the good of God can be reduced to the status of a supernatural person, or that evil can be embodied in a supernatural being. Rather, each individual has her own **relationship** to the forces of good and evil. That relationship depends upon the level of spiritual awareness that an individual has attained.

Angels and Archangels

The Edgar Cayce readings confirm that there are hierarchical levels of spiritual beings. In Reading 5749-3, Cayce was specifically asked to address the topic of "Angels and Archangels and How They Help Humanity." This reading provides a wealth of information on the nature of angels.

> "With the bringing into creation the manifested forms, there came that which has been, is, and ever will be, the spirit realm and its attributes - designated as angels and archangels. They are the spiritual manifestations in the spirit world of those attributes that the developing forces accredit to the One Source..."

The reading goes on to say that they operate under divine law and are synonymous with what humans call the laws of the universe.

> "They are as the laws of the universe; as is
> Michael the lord of the Way, NOT the Way
> but the lord of the Way..."

Reading 5749-3 also tells us that angelic beings manifest in the material world and serve to help us develop both mentally and spiritually.

> "...that may be seen in material planes
> through the influences that may aid in
> development of the mental and spiritual
> forces through an experience - or in the
> acquiring of knowledge that may aid in the
> intercourse one with another."

It would seem that the old folktale is true. Each person has a guardian angel that guides and guards him. "As indicated, ever the guardian angel stands before the throne of God - for each individual." (3189-3) The purpose of our guardian angel is to protect and guide us as we make choices during our earthly sojourn.

> "...each soul in its walks in the earth has
> its angel...And these are always ready to
> guide, to guard, if the soul will but put
> itself in the position in material things to
> be guided by spiritual truths." (531-2)

The readings also identify some of these celestial beings by name, including the archangels Michael, Gabriel, Ariel, and Halaliel. The readings describe Michael as "an archangel that stands before the throne of the Father...Michael is the lord or the guard of the change that comes in every soul that seeks the way..." (262-28) As the guardian of the way, Michael acts as a protective presence to each seeker who is striving to progress along the spiritual path.

Gabriel, traditionally thought of as God's messenger, is also mentioned in several readings. The readings call Gabriel "the announcer" and confirm the role that he played in the Biblical stories where he is portrayed as announcing John the Baptist's birth to Elizabeth, and Jesus' birth to Mary and Joseph.

Another archangel mentioned in the readings was Halaliel, who is described as "one who from the beginning has been a leader of the heavenly host, who has defied Ariel" (254-83) and who "was with those in the beginning who warred with those that separated themselves and became as naught." (262-56) Ariel, in turn, is cited as being a companion of Lucifer, who "made for the disputing of the influences in the experiences of Adam in the Garden." (262-57)

One of the most interesting things to happen during the readings occurred when two of the archangels noted above spoke through Cayce. One being who spoke through Cayce identified himself as Michael. The other identified himself as Halaliel.

The archangel Michael spoke through Cayce on eight occasions, four of which occurred during readings given for the "Search for God" Study Group reference material. On each occasion Michael identified himself as "I, Michael" and delivered a brief warning or admonition that cautioned the listeners to stay true to the way of the Lord. The following is a typical example of one of Michael's warnings:

> "HARK! O YE CHILDREN OF MEN! BOW THINE HEADS, YE SONS OF MEN. FOR THE GLORY OF THE LORD IS THINE. WILL YE BE FAITHFUL TO THE TRUST THAT IS PUT IN EACH OF YOU! KNOW IN WHOM YE HAVE BELIEVED! KNOW THAT HE IS LORD OF ALL, AND HIS WORD FAILEST NOT TO THEM THAT

ARE FAITHFUL DAY BY DAY: FOR I, MICHAEL, WOULD PROTECT THOSE THAT SEEK TO KNOW HIS FACE!" (262-29)

Each time Michael spoke through Cayce, those present would notice a change not only in the tone of his voice, but also in its volume. Michael spoke with a loud, booming voice, which would literally shake the bodies of those present and rattle the dishes in the next room. His brief presence always had a profound effect on the listeners, moving them to tears and creating the impression that they had indeed been in the presence of the divine. Michael's infrequent appearances appeared to have served the purpose of delivering a warning to those present at the reading.

Another entity that called himself Halaliel spoke through Cayce in 1934. He offered his services as a channel and source of information. The readings that came through Halaliel focused primarily on future earth changes. Halaliel's appearance caused much concern among the members of the Search for God Study Group for whom the readings were being given.

Eventually a majority of the group members decided to reject Halaliel's offer to serve as a channel and chose instead to rely upon Cayce's ability to directly access the Universal Mind, for they believed this was the highest expression of unity consciousness. Following their decision, Halaliel did not appear again.

The number of times that these two archangels spoke through Cayce is very rare, however, considering the 14,000-plus readings that were given over forty-plus years. These occurrences should be considered as exceptions rather than the rule. They happened for specific purposes and were not the normal way in which Cayce obtained his information from the Universal Consciousness.

The Brotherhood of Masters

The readings also indicate that there is another order of celestial beings, in addition to angels and archangels, who have never experienced physical consciousness in the way the soul has. The readings call these beings "the masters."

> "To be sure, there are those consciousnesses or awarenesses that have not participated in nor been a part of earth's PHYSICAL consciousness; as the angels, the archangels, *the masters* [italics for author's emphasis] to whom there has been attainment, and to those influences that have prepared the way." (5755-2)

The masters seem to be a group of celestial beings that have never incarnated on the physical plane. They provide help and guidance to humanity through spiritual means. The guidance and messages they bring are available to all those who open their minds and desire to hear the truth. Reading 254-83 provided a great deal of insight into these beings. A portion of the reading is quoted below.

> "Yes, we - from the source of all knowledge that is promised in Him - salute thee, and give that which will be helpful to those who seek to be in the ministry of those influences and forces that make for more and more awareness of the divine in each and every soul...Then, from the heights of those experiences, those hierarchies in the earth and in the air, we come as messengers of truth to those who will hear, and

> question...from the universal forces that
> are acceptable and accessible to those that
> in earnestness OPEN their minds, their
> souls, to the wonderful words of truth and
> light...MESSENGERS from the higher
> forces that may manifest from the Throne
> of grace itself."

From various references scattered throughout the
readings, we see that these beings have played an active
role in human affairs even before the time of recorded
history. They have guided all of the "Great Teachers"
who have left their mark upon humankind. They have
been present during critical times and key events that
mark humanity's progress across the generations.

It is possible that many of these masters are souls
such as we are. They made the choice not to incarnate
on the earth plane, and therefore have never departed
from a unity consciousness with the Creative Force. If
this interpretation is true, we are indeed their brethren;
this explains why they are committed to helping us
return to our original state of unity with God. It is also
likely that the masters are the source of references to the
bene ha-elohim, the heavenly host and "sons of God"
that are mentioned in Scripture.

According to the readings, the masters are members
of what is called the "Great White Brotherhood." The
term "white" does not have any racial significance; rather
it refers to the color white in the sense of the "white light"
of truth. The Brotherhood also appears to include souls
who have manifested in physical form and successfully
completed the cycle of incarnations on the earth plane.

In the esoteric traditions, the Great White
Brotherhood extends back to Egyptian times and refers to
a group dedicated to the preservation of spiritual truths.
They include Hermes Trismegistus, King Solomon,
Pythagoras, Plato, and other teachers of the ancient

mystery religions. The Great Pyramid at Gizeh is identified as their "hall of initiates" where students of these Adepts would face their final trials and testing.

Reading 5748-5 indicates that both John the Baptist and Jesus of Nazareth took their final initiation in the Great Pyramid. "In this same pyramid did the Great Initiate, the Master, take those last of the Brotherhood degrees with John, the forerunner of Him, at that place." Other readings indicate that Jesus of Nazareth, upon completion of the cycle of his incarnations on the earth plane, attained to the Christ Consciousness and is now acknowledged as the "Master of masters." A number of readings contained references regarding others members of the Brotherhood who were present on the earth plane at the time the reading was given.

Spirit Forces

In addition to angelic beings, the readings also speak of "spirit forces." Some of these spirit forces may be different orders of creation, entities that have not entered into the material plane but who may manifest in physical form from time to time. These beings are likely the source of folktales about fairies, gnomes, pixies, and brownies (refer to Reading 1265-3).

Sometimes these entities are sent to us as guides for a specific purpose. In this respect, they act much in the same manner as a guardian angel. "All guides, whether spiritual or material, have the power to direct and influence their subjects." (4348-1) Other spirit forces may not be as helpful as those sent to us by the Creator, as indicated in excerpts from two readings presented below:

> "There are those influences from without the veil that seek - seek - that they may find an expression, that they may still be

> a portion of this evolution in the earth,
> not considering their present estate. And
> these bring turmoil, strife." (1132-5)

> "For the angels of light only use material
> things for emblems, while the angels of
> death use these as to lures that may carry
> men's souls away." (1159-1)

The first reading seems to refer to souls who have passed beyond the veil—the earth plane. Although they are now in spirit form, they seek to continue their connection with the physical world. The second reading is interesting in that it clearly speaks of "angels" and yet associates these angels with death and temptation. This is similar to the earlier Jewish concept that angels could bring bad tidings as well as good.

The readings further indicate that the type of spirit forces we attract is related to the purpose or ideal we hold.

> "As is seen...there are ever about those in
> the flesh in the earth's plane those
> desiring to communicate with those in the
> earth plane, attracted by the act, intent
> and purport of the individual, or by the
> act, intent, purport, of that entity in the
> spirit plane." (900-330)

This reading demonstrates the importance of the ideal we hold in mind. If your consciousness is focused solely on material and selfish motives, you will attract negative spiritual influences that may retard your spiritual growth. If you keep your consciousness focused on spiritual ideals, however, you will attract beneficial spiritual influences that will aid in your spiritual development.

The readings also indicate that even those who hold to the highest spiritual ideal can be subject to interference by forces that seek to deter them from the spiritual path. Reading 2897-4 tells of a continual battle between the archangel Michael and these forces. A question posed during the reading asked why Cayce was "surrounded by such wrong vibrations and entities in this great work?" The answer given spoke of this continuing battle:

> "For there has been the continued battle with those forces as Michael fought WITH over the body of Moses. He that leads, or WOULD direct, is continually beset by the forces that WOULD undermine."

Reading 5749-3 also addresses this issue: [Michael] "disputed with the influence of evil as to the way of the spirit of the teacher or director in his entrance through the outer door." This reading refers to the story told in Jude 1:9, in which the archangel Michael contended with the devil for the body of Moses upon his death.

Satan, Prince of Demons

While the readings contain numerous references to angelic beings and spirit forces, they do not contain much information about beings referred to in other traditions as "demons." A word search of the readings shows that fifteen readings contain the word "demon." Thirteen of these are references to Biblical stories of demons cast out by Jesus of Nazareth while the other two use the word "demon" in a general way rather than in reference to specific beings. The readings regarding the demons cast out by Jesus indicate that these stories are real, thus implying that demons do exist.

The readings do contain a good deal of information about the Devil, or Satan, and the role he played in the origin of evil, both on the spiritual and material planes. The reading given below describes his activity in spirit.

> "In the beginning, celestial beings. We have first the Son, then the other sons or celestial beings that are given their force and power.   Hence that force which rebelled in the unseen forces (or in spirit) that came into activity, was that influence which has been called Satan, the Devil, the Serpent;   they   are   One.   That   of REBELLION!" (262-52)

Reading 262-89 contains more information about this entity and describes his activities in the material plane.

> "It has been understood by most of those who have attained to a consciousness of the various presentations of good and evil in manifested forms, as we have indicated, that the prince of this world, Satan, Lucifer, the Devil - *as a soul* [author's italics   for   emphasis]   -   made   those necessities, as it were, of the consciousness in materiality; that man might - or that the soul   might   -   become   aware   of   its separation from the God-force."

The implications of these readings are astounding, yet the meaning is clear.   First, they confirm the existence of the being known as Satan.   Second, they identify him as a soul whose activities were necessary in order for humanity to become aware of its separation from God.   According to the readings, Satan is not a celestial being with supernatural powers, nor a mighty archangel who had fallen from grace.   Satan is an **individual soul**, as we all are.

Satan: Fallen Angel or Wayward Soul?

Initially, I thought the idea of Satan as a soul to be somewhat strange. As I considered this concept more closely, however, I realized that it did indeed make sense. Further, it actually helped explain a number of inconsistencies in traditional theological thought.

The concept of Satan as a soul is not really remarkable, especially when we consider that Jesus of Nazareth, who became the Christ, was also a soul. The readings make it clear that Jesus was a man (individual soul) while the Christ was the spiritual pattern (the consciousness). Jesus was the physical incarnation of the soul who, through patience, understanding, and the practice of unconditional love, attuned his will to be one with God's will at all times. He manifested a total awareness of his divine heritage and unity with the Creative Force to the point of being able to overcome the physical death of the body itself. He thus attained the Christ Consciousness.

The idea of Satan as a soul also coincides nicely with the original Jewish concept of satan [note the lowercase "s"] as a member of the *bene ha-elohim*, which translates to "sons of God." As discussed earlier, the *bene ha-elohim* were members of the heavenly host. They were distinguished from the *ma'lakhim Yahweh*, or angels of God, who acted as His servants and emissaries.

It is interesting to note that the phrase "sons of God" is frequently used in the readings to refer to the group of souls who came to earth and yet retained the memory of their divine origin. It should also be remembered that the concept of Satan as a fallen angel did not appear until much later in Jewish history, primarily as a result of the Persian influence.

As a soul, Satan would have possessed the birthright of free will. The power of choice, manifested through the freedom of the will, is one of the basic principles explained in the readings. No other order of God's creation possesses free will. It is the birthright of the soul alone. "For, will is that birthright to each soul which makes the difference between man and the rest of creation." (2246-1) Angels and archangels, however, are traditionally depicted as servants and messengers of God, an order of creation created to do God's bidding. Since they do not possess free will they must follow Divine Will.

Knowing that angels are obedient servants of God who do not possess free will, I always wondered how Satan could have rebelled against God of his own accord. I wondered how a being created for the sole purpose of serving God could exercise an attribute that he did not possess. This is why some scholars have speculated that Satan acts as an agent of God, and that his activities in the material world are somehow a part of a divine plan.

When I began the research for this book, I would not have been surprised to find some reference in the readings stating that Satan, through his rebellious actions, was actually carrying out the will of God. I expected him to be portrayed as God's agent in the unfolding of a divine plan we did not completely comprehend. However, the fact that the readings state Satan is a soul who possesses free will answers the question as to how he could rebel against the Creative Force.

The readings go on to tell the story of how Satan was actively involved in the origin of evil, both in the spirit realm and in the material world. We will discuss this story further in the next chapter.

7
The Origin of Evil

> *The lie is the specific evil which man*
> *has introduced into nature.*
> Martin Buber

In the Cayce readings, the origin of evil is related to four other issues: the creation of the soul, the misuse of free will, the creation of the material dimension, and the being known as Satan. In order to understand the Cayce perspective on good and evil, we must also appreciate what the readings have to tell us about these matters.

The Creation Story

The Edgar Cayce readings tell us that in the beginning was Spirit, a vast expanse of discerning energy, occupying all space and time. This Spirit exists as pure energy. Its essence is the positive and negative forces—the forces of attraction and repulsion—that exist at the atomic level of activity. The movement or vibration of these atomic forces is the creative power that exists within universe. Consider the following excerpts taken from Reading 262-52:

> "In the manifestation of all power, force, motion, vibration, that which impels, that which detracts, is in its essence of one force, one source, in its elemental form...God, the first cause, the first principle, the first movement, IS! That's the beginning!...In the beginning there was the force of attraction and the force that repelled...Yet this very movement that

> separates the forces in atomic influence is
> the first cause, or the manifestation of that
> called God in the material plane!...Then, as
> it gathers of positive-negative forces in
> their activity, whether it be of one element
> or realm or another, it becomes magnified
> in its force or sources through the
> universe. Hence we find worlds, suns,
> stars, nebulae, and whole solar systems
> MOVING from a first cause."

As the activity of the atomic forces varies, it creates
a different manifestation. The essence of the energy
force or Spirit, however, remains the same. Differences
in the vibrational activity of the atomic forces create
molecules, cells, and the basic elements that make up
the universe. We see this expressed in Reading 5753-1
as follows.

> "Hence in the various spheres that man
> sees (that are demonstrated, manifested,
> in and before self) even in a material
> world, all forces, all activities, are a
> manifestation...Because an atom, a matter,
> a form, is changed does not mean that the
> essence, the source or the spirit of it has
> changed; only in its form of manifestation,
> and NOT in its relation with the first
> cause."

This Spirit thus embraces the total life energy and
elemental forms of all existence, spiritual, mental, and
material. This Spirit is the "I AM THAT I AM," the
eternal Creative Force and Universal Mind that we call
God. It is the First Cause of all being.

The readings tell us that God sought self-expression
through creation and also desired companionship. The

First Cause of creation was God's (Spirit's) desire for companionship:

> "The first cause was, that the created would be the companion for the Creator; that it, the creature, would - through its manifestations in the activity of that given unto the creature - show itself to be not only worthy of, but companionable to, the Creator." (5753-1)

We were first created in spirit; our true nature is that of a spiritual being. "For in the beginning God said, 'Let there be light.' Ye, [5367], are one of those sparks of light with all the ability of creation, with all the knowledge of God." (5367-1)

While the spirit is the spark of the Creative Force contained within us, the soul can be thought of as an individualized expression of that energy. "The soul is an individual, individuality, that may grow to be one with, or separate from, the whole. The spirit is the impelling influence of infinity, or the one creative source, force, that is manifest." (5749-3) Souls were created when the Creative Force (Spirit) extended itself to create companions and co-creators. "Hence, as He moved, souls - portions of Himself - came into being." (263-13)

In order to create a true companion possessing co-creative abilities God determined that its creation must possess the same attributes as the Creator. The soul was therefore given the faculty of free will as its birthright. Reading 262-56 tells us,

> "The Creator, in seeking to find...a being worthy of companionship, realized that such a being would result only from a free will exercising its divine inheritance and through its own efforts find its Maker."

While God knew that free will was necessary to enable the soul to be a true co-creative companion, He also knew that the soul could choose to exercise that free will in a way contrary to Divine Will. "Man alone is given that birthright of free will. He alone may defy his God!" (5757-1) God therefore also endowed the soul with the faculty of development so that it might learn from experience.

The faculty of development ensured that once a soul made a choice, it would learn from the consequences of that choice. "Hence the development is through the planes of experience that an entity may become one WITH the first cause...in whatever state, place or plane of development the entity is passing." (5749-3)

The Separation in Spirit

According to the readings, all souls existed in harmonious unity with the Creative Force at the moment of creation. Yet each soul also possessed a sense of self in that it was an individualized expression of that force. We can only surmise what existence must have been like following our spiritual creation. What a glorious time it must have been as the beauty and order of all creation was set before us. We could travel through different realms of consciousness and experience all that the universe had to offer. With just a thought, we could bring our own creations into being.

To truly be as God (not God but "as God") it was necessary for the soul to have the opportunity to know God, and also to know its opposite or "not-God." The soul, therefore, was given the ability to experience both God (unity) and not-God (separation).

Consider Reading 262-56, which states, "Thus, to make the choice really a Divine one caused the existence of states of consciousness, that would indeed tax the free will of a soul; thus light and darkness."

At some point, souls, through the birthright of free will, erred. A soul had the erroneous thought of separation and believed itself to be separate from God. "Hence the separation, and light and darkness. Darkness, that it had separated - that a *soul had separated itself* [author's italics for emphasis] from the light." (262-56)

This self-induced separation first occurred in spirit. As Reading 1602-3 tells us, "...the separation - that as caused the separation of souls from the universal consciousness - came not in the sphere of materiality first, but in that of spirit." It occurred long before the material dimension had come into being. "As has been given, error or separation began before there appeared what we know as the Earth, the Heavens; or before Space was manifested." (262-115)

The readings refer to this separation as an act of rebellion born of selfishness—the selfish desire to be something other than what one was created to be. "Then what is this Spirit of Rebellion, what is this Spirit of Hate? What is this Spirit of Self-Indulgence? What is this Spirit that makes men afraid? SELFISHNESS!" (262-114)

Souls rebelled in the sense that they chose to go against the evolutionary impulse of First Cause. They did so by desiring to be other than what they were created to be and to use their creative abilities in ways contrary to that originally intended, "What separated spirit from its first cause, or [what] causes good and evil? Desire! DESIRE!" (5752-3)

While the soul was given an opportunity to experience a state of separation, the error committed by the soul was to believe that the separation consciousness was its reality. This was the first error of perception. A soul who **accepted** the separation as reality and **chose to remain** in this state of consciousness denied the nature of its true self and the purpose for which it was created. The soul thus lost the knowledge of its relationship to God.

It is possible that the being known as Satan may very well have been the first soul to explore a different realm of consciousness by entertaining the erroneous thought of separation. *A Course in Miracles*[24] describes this event as the moment when a soul had the erroneous thought of separation and "forgot to laugh."

> "In the beginning, celestial beings. We have first the Son, then the other sons or celestial beings that are given their force and power. Hence that force which rebelled in the unseen forces (or in spirit) that came into activity, was that influence which has been called Satan, the Devil, the Serpent; they are One. That of REBELLION!" (262-52)

The souls that chose to follow Satan's example became channels for the expression of this spirit of rebellion, this spirit of evil. As Reading 262-119 explains, "Understandest thou? Then, what did it mean? Only that such channels *[author's note: the souls that rebelled]* offered ways and means for the expression of those influences claimed by Satan, the Devil, the Evil One, as his...."

The separation in consciousness and the division it created is the source of myths about the casting out of Satan and his followers from heaven. These stories are symbolic memories of the chaos that followed the first error of perception. Much of the symbolism in the Book of Enoch tells of this separation, with references to rebellious angels as "fallen stars." In the Book of Adam and Eve, Satan desires to be like God himself, setting his seat above God's throne. A variation of this story is told in the Secrets of Enoch, when Satanail, in arrogance and pride, "conceived an impossible thought"25 that he could set his throne above the clouds and become equal in stature to God. For this error, he and his followers were held in darkness, separated from the presence of God. The common themes in these myths are a direct reflection of the separation in spirit that is described in the readings. One major difference is that in these stories Satan and his followers are given the status of angels rather than souls.

The first error in perception and the separation consciousness that resulted led to chaos and conflict in the spiritual plane—the beginning of the war between good and evil. "Then there came that as sought for self-indulgence, self-glorification; and there was the beginning of warring among themselves for activity - STILL in Spirit...." (262-114)

In response to the question, "What is meant here by the war in heaven between Michael and the Devil?," Cayce gave the following answer:

> "As has just been given, as is understood by those here, there is first - as is the spiritual concept - the spiritual rebellion, before it takes mental or physical form. This warring is illustrated there by the war between the Lord of the Way *[author's note: the Archangel Michael]* and the Lord of Darkness - or the Lord of Rebellion." (281-33)

An Alternate Plan

The Creative Force, however, was not content to accept the chaos that resulted from the souls' error of perception. Rather, God desired that no soul should perish and therefore put an alternative plan into action. The readings tell us that God devised a plan whereby all

souls were given the opportunity to correct their error
of perception and recognize the truth of their being and
their unity with the Creative Force.   Consider the
following excerpt from Reading 262-56,

> "He has not willed that any soul should
> perish, but from the beginning has
> prepared a way of escape...Bringing into
> being the various phases that the soul may
> find in its manifested forms the
> consciousness and awareness of its
> separation, and itself, by that through
> which it passes in all the various spheres of
> its awareness."

This reading tells us that God prepared a plan (a way
of escape), designed to bring different levels of
consciousness (various phases) to our attention while in
physical form (find in its manifested forms) so that we
might become aware of our self-induced separation and
the nature of our true being.   This plan unfolds as we
learn, grow, and develop in all planes of existence (various
spheres).

The nucleus of this plan was the creation of the
material dimension.[26] While in the nebulous world of
spirit, the soul could not easily understand the
separation (darkness) it had created between itself and
the Creative Force (the light).   Once in matter, the soul
would experience a slowing of its vibratory rate so that
it might come to see the difference between its
erroneous state of separation and its original state of
unity with the Creative Force. Reading 262-56 explains
this as follows:

> "by becoming aware in a material world IS
> – or was – the only manner or way
> through which spiritual forces might

> become aware of their separation from
> the spiritual atmosphere, the spiritual
> surroundings, of the Maker."

To help the soul recognize the separation it had created, the Creative Force modified its original plan that intended for the soul to remain in sprit. Through the creation of the material dimension, the soul now had an opportunity to understand the separation.

Opportunity in the Material World

The readings describe the creation of the material dimension as a breathtaking event. They speak of the time when the morning stars sang together and the whispering winds and rushing waters proclaimed the coming of the souls' indwelling in materiality. Reading 3508-1 describes this creation.

> "God moved, the spirit came into
> activity...In this light came creation of
> that which in the earth came to be
> matter...until there are the heavens and
> all the constellations, the stars, the
> universe as it is known - or sought to be
> known by individual soul-entities in the
> material plane."

Spirit pushed into matter and entered the three-dimensional physical world, a world created to help us experience the effects of the separation so we might see how far we had moved from the light. The earth we entered was a world of polar opposites—positive and negative electrical charges, male and female, and light and darkness. Each sojourn on the earth plane was designed to provide the soul with the **opportunity** to experience as many of these differences—polar opposites—as possible, and through **comparison** come to realize the difference between unity and separation. Consider the following example of how this can happen in the material world.

> "As one is passing there may be a flash of a shadow from a plane, a cloud, a bird, or that which makes one more aware of the light; though one may itself be wholly in the light...One becomes aware by comparison in the material plane." (262-56)

If we are standing in the sunlight of the noonday sun, our eyesight becomes accustomed to its intensity; we may not even think of its brightness. Yet if a bird flies overhead and casts a shadow, we not only become aware of the sun's intensity, we also become aware of the shadow. It is because of the difference between the two that we better understand both.

Conversely, if we stand in the darkness of a cloud-covered, starless night, we see only the depth of its darkness. If a shooting star suddenly appears and for a moment illuminates even a small portion of the sky, we become aware of both the light and the darkness.

It is through such comparisons while on earth that we truly become conscious of the difference between our separation from the Creative Force and unity with the spiritual source of all creative power. The material world was thus created to afford the soul the opportunity to recognize the separation it had created, correct its first error of perception, and rediscover its true nature and relationship with God.

We were to reclaim our birthright as co-creators with God by exercising our creative abilities in accordance with Divine Will. "In man's advent into a material world is an opportunity for the material manifestation of that which is builded by the individual soul through its activity in the various spheres of consciousness..." (262-50) Life on earth allowed us to have the opportunity for "paralleling, correlating, cooperating, bringing into existence the effects of using all experience presented for the development of the soul."27

Once in the material dimension, however, souls again lost sight of their true nature and purpose. In expressing their creative abilities in the material world, they came to believe that they were the Creative Force itself rather than beings capable of directing the creative energy that flowed through them. This was the second error of perception.

> "When this first cause comes into man's experience in the present realm he becomes confused, in that he appears to have an influence upon this force or power in directing same. Certainly! Much, though, in the manner as the reflection of light in a mirror." (262-52)

The readings tell of three soul groups or root races (see Appendix C) that entered the earth plane in an ordered succession. As each soul group entered materiality, it fell prey to the second error of perception. This fueled the fires of a separation consciousness, as souls, now in physical form, saw themselves as individual entities, separate not only from God, but also separate from one another. Through free will these souls began to express their creative abilities in ways that were contrary to Divine Will and physical law.

> "Remember, as given, the earth is that speck, that part of creation where souls projected themselves into matter, and thus brought that conscious awareness of

themselves entertaining the ability of
creating without those forces of the spirit
of truth." (5755-2)

Souls within each group were also intrigued by the
many physical sensations animal bodies were capable of
experiencing. Many chose to project themselves deeper
into matter for increasing periods of time in an attempt
to experience more of the "earthy" sensations common
to the animal kingdom. These souls not only
abandoned their own path of spiritual development, but
also interfered with the natural evolution of various
animal species on earth. The co-creative abilities of the
soul were misused for selfish purposes contrary to
Divine Will.

Within each group of souls that entered the earth
plane there were those that remained true to their
divine nature as well as those that chose to separate
themselves from God. The division in thought, purpose,
and ideal between these two factions, a division that
first began in spirit, continued upon the earth. "Hence
the continued warring that is ever present in materiality
or in the flesh, or the warring - as is termed - between
the flesh and the devil, or the warring between those
influences of good and evil." (262-89)

Satan's Role on Earth

Just as Satan was active in the spirit realm, he was
again active on earth. In Reading 262-119, Cayce was
asked to comment on "The devil and satan, which
deceiveth the whole world, he was SENT out into the
earth." Cayce responded,

"Did He not - the Christ, the Maker - say
this over and over again? that so long as
spite, selfishness, evil desires, evil

> communications were manifested, they
> would give the channels through which
> THAT spirit called satan, devil, Lucifer,
> Evil One, might work?"

I interpret this reading to mean that as long as there
are those that choose to exercise free will in pursuit of self
there will be an opportunity for the spirit of Satan—the
spirit of selfishness—to manifest as evil on earth.

Reading 262-89 goes one step further and implies
that Satan may play a very important role in our spiritual
development.

> "...the prince of this world, Satan, Lucifer,
> the Devil - as a soul - made those
> necessities, as it were, of the consciousness
> in materiality; that man might - or that the
> soul might - *become aware of its
> separation* [author's italics for emphasis]
> from the God-force."

The clear inference contained in this reading is that
Satan's presence in the physical world is a necessary
part of our spiritual development so that we might
realize we had separated ourselves from God. Might it
be possible that Satan's activities on earth were in
accordance with a divine plan designed to illuminate
our errors of perception and help us recognize the
separation we had created? If so, Satan acts less as an
adversary of God and more as an agent of His will. This
means that it is not Satan per se that is to blame for the
evil we see around us, but rather it is the desires and
activities of the soul that allow evil to flourish upon the
earth.

8

The Reality of Evil

*...evil is a constant threat for it has
the power to possess and destroy the human soul
or extinguish our lives through war, disease, crime.*
John A. Sanford, <u>Evil, The Shadow Side of Reality</u>

As we learned in the last chapter, God did not create evil. It came into being as a result of the activities of the soul. As reading 479-1 states, "TRUE, sin and error is not of GOD - save through His sons that BROUGHT error, through selfishness, into the experience of the souls of men." This happened first in spirit as told in Reading 262-56, "The separation or turning away brought evil." It happened again as we entered material form. "Yet, with the setting of those alterations there came good and that opposite from good (to know good) into the material manifestations." (262-52) It was the self-induced separation and the consequent misuse of creative abilities that brought evil into existence.

We might say that good and evil can be seen as different levels of awareness or states of consciousness. Good is the awareness of one's true spiritual nature and relationship to God. It is unity consciousness with the Creative Force. When a soul entity acknowledges its oneness with the Creative Force and applies its creative abilities in accordance with Divine Order, good manifests. Since it is a direct expression of the Creative Force, good exists as an eternal aspect of creation.

Evil is the lack of awareness of one's true self and the self's relation to God. It is a separation consciousness. When a soul rejects the knowledge of its unity with God and chooses to misapply its creative abilities in defiance of Divine Will, chaos and evil result. Evil is not a separate power apart from God; it is a rebellious use of creative power. Since evil is the misuse of creative ability, it is not real in the sense that it is not eternal.[28] "For good alone lives on. Evil perisheth with the day. Good is of God and thus eternal." (1662-2)

There is an inherent danger, however, in thinking that evil is simply a lack of something. There is a distinction between the rebellious thoughts of separation and the power that flows from them. Evil is more than a lack of spiritual awareness. It is more than just a state of consciousness. Evil is **a misapplication of the soul's creative power**, and that power is very strong because it is the power of the Creative Force itself.

Visionary theologian, and proponent of creation spirituality, Matthew Fox recognizes this fact and has written extensively about evil and sin being "misdirected love" flowing through the chakras. When used correctly, in accordance with Divine Will, our creative powers are capable of bringing worlds into being. When used incorrectly, in defiance of Divine Will, they can cause indescribable suffering, chaos, and destruction. The power and influence of evil is very real, both in the heavens and on the earth.

The Effects of Separation Consciousness

It is far beyond the scope of this book to discuss the many ways in which evil has manifested on earth. Any book on human history will tell this story. The problem with history, however, is that our own perspective affects the way we perceive historic events. One person's hero may be another person's traitor.

Rather than recount the chronicle of human history, I believe we may gain more insight into the manifestation of evil by examining the ways a separation consciousness leads to various life perspectives that cause a person to create evil. A life perspective is our fundamental attitude toward life itself. It is the motivating force that determines how a person perceives her relationship to self, to others, and to God. It embraces certain values, ideals, and principles that determine the way we relate to all aspects of life. It thus directs our behavior.

A separation consciousness leads to the formation of three basic life perspectives based on beliefs that prevent us from feeling a connection to anyone or anything. These are indifference, specialness, and fear. All the various evils[29] recognized by humanity throughout the ages are rooted in the erroneous perceptions of these life perspectives. They result in behaviors, historically called sin, that are life-threatening rather than life-supporting. Sin is defined here in broad terms that cut across cultural and religious boundaries. Keep in mind that there are many different ways to define sin. The classification used here reflects the personal preferences of the author.

The First Error of Perception	The Second Error of Perception
Indifference	**Specialness**
Sins of Omission *Apathy* *Despair* *Injustice* *Denial*	**Sins of Dualism** *Arrogance* *Envy* *Resentment* *Greed* *Gluttony*
Fear	
Sins of Hate *Anger* *Violence* *Cruelty* *Sadism*	

Table 2. Perception, Evil, and Sin

Indifference and Inaction

Refer to Table 2, *Perception, Evil, and Sin*, during the following discussion. Indifference is a life perspective that is rooted in the first error of perception. A person who believes he is separate from the rest of the world lacks emotional enthusiasm or the ability to care about anyone or anything. He may not even care about himself. People who live from a perspective of indifference consistently choose the course of inaction.

Outwardly, inaction appears to be a lack of activity or a failure to do something. Inaction, however, actually implies prior action, the prior action being the **decision** not to do something. The failure to act does have an effect and can lead to more serious results than what we choose to do. In fact, the Edgar Cayce readings say that to know and not do, is sin.

Indifference leads a person to commit what have traditionally been called the "sins of omission." These include apathy, despair, injustice, and denial. While in today's world we don't normally think of sins of omission as being evil, spiritual leaders throughout history have warned us against the dangers they bring. St. Thomas Aquinas believed that sins of omission are greater than those we commit. Hildegard of Bingen said that apathy caused the soul to be "weakened by the coldness of indifference and neglect." St. John Chrysostom believed it was despair that casts us into hell. When in the grip of despair, the soul gives up hope. Despair allows us to do wicked things because nothing matters anymore.

Injustice is the lack of passion for justice or for caring about anything at all. It also flows from apathy, because without zeal we have no energy for the struggle, no willingness to fight for what we believe to be right. Denial is a willful ignorance, a repression of something we know. It is a deliberate ignoring of the truth. It keeps us out of touch with our deepest feelings, the feelings a person must integrate in order to become whole. It prevents us from seeing ourselves as we truly are.

The dangers of apathy and the sins of omission were called to the world's attention by Reverend Martin Niemoller, a German Protestant pastor and head of the anti-Nazi Confessing Church. During the height of Nazism in Germany he was arrested for malicious attacks against the state and spent seven years in the Dachau and Sachsenhausen concentration camps. Released by the Allies in 1945, he penned this moving and often quoted poem,

> "In Germany, they first came for the communists, and I didn't speak up because I wasn't a communist. Then they came for the Jews, and I didn't speak up because I wasn't a Jew. Then they came for the trade unionists, and I didn't speak up because I wasn't a trade unionist. Then they came for the Catholics and I didn't speak up because I wasn't a Catholic. Then they came for me—and by that time there was nobody left to speak up."

Elie Weisel, a survivor of the Holocaust, who has dedicated his life to keeping the memory of those events alive, shares a similar view.

> "I swore never to be silent whenever or wherever human beings endure suffering and humiliation. We must always take sides; neutrality helps the oppressor, never the victim. Silence encourages the tormentor, never the tormented."

Indifference may very well be the most dangerous of all life perspectives. It is dangerous in the sense that although inaction appears harmless, the consequences that result from inaction can have devastating effects, for it is our very inaction that allows evil to exist. Our sins of omission—apathy, despair, injustice, and denial—allow evil to flourish. Indifference may appear to be benign but in truth it opens the door for evil and invites it to enter into our lives.

Specialness and Dualism

The perspective of specialness stems from the second error of perception whereby a person believes she is the source of creative power and therefore special and more deserving than others. *A Course in Miracles* teaches that specialness is the great lie that continues to foster a separation consciousness. So long as we consider ourselves to be special, we consider ourselves to be different from those who are not special. As long as we are different in some way, we cannot be united.

Specialness leads to the sins of dualism. The sins of dualism include arrogance, greed, addiction or gluttony, envy or covetousness, and resentment. They cause harm not only to others, but also to self as they further estrange a person from other human beings.

Arrogance refers to a type of unhealthy pride whereby one tries to appropriate something to which he has no legitimate claim. Arrogance results in feelings of superiority over another person perceived to be different, whether the differences are individual, ethnic, or religious in nature.

Greed flows from arrogance. It prompts a person to take whatever she can, justly or unjustly. St. Aquinas said greed causes us to look for the infinite in the finite; we look for satisfaction in objects that cannot satisfy. It arises from an erroneous belief in lack. We believe that if we do not take it all, we will be caught short. We therefore always seek more, even at the expense of others.

Addiction or gluttony occurs when we are out of balance and desire itself overtakes reason. We lose control as the addiction becomes the primary motivating force in our lives. It is one-sided in that it allows for nothing else to share its place. Eventually the self is destroyed as well.

Envy is defined as feeling sadness over another's good fortune, feeling sorrow over another's blessings. It gives rise to rivalry, mistrust, and malice, all of which separate and divide. Envy breeds resentment. Resentment is anger oriented to the present. Resentment occurs when we hold on to a hurt that festers and grows until we see no other option but to seek revenge. It is a powerful force that sets us on the road to hate.

Fear and Hate

The life perspective of fear results when a person truly embraces a separation consciousness. The sense of isolation a person feels in this state, combined with the belief of specialness, causes him to see life as a continual battle against a world he feels is inferior. He feels justified in striking out against the world because it is the source of his fear.

The person who evaluates life from a separation consciousness strikes out in hatred because we hate those things we fear. Hatred is irrational anger directed indiscriminately against anyone or anything. The person who acts out of hatred feels justified in doing so because he feels superior to what he intends to destroy.

The ability to engage in actions based on hatred is made possible by the process of objectification. Objectification occurs when we reduce a living being to the status of an object. We "depersonalize" the individual and make her less than human. We can only objectify someone if we see ourselves as separate and distinct from that person. Objectification allows us to justify immoral treatment of that person since we cease to see her as an individual with feelings and rights and instead see that being as a means to our own ends.

Objectification is the first step that enables us to commit the sins of hate: violence, cruelty, and sadism. Together, hatred and objectification work hand-in-hand to allow us to overlook justice and harm others without regard for the consequences.

The most extreme forms of violence are cruelty and sadism. Both are a grievous misuse of our imaginative and creative powers. Cruelty is the imposition of pain, physical, mental, or emotional, upon another in order to cause anguish and fear. According to psychologist Erich Fromm, the core of sadism is the compulsion to control others. Both can be imposed on an individual level or on a global level, such as occurs in war. In fact, many wars have been characterized by the institutionalized brutality that allows an entire nation to commit sadistic atrocities upon others.

The Power of Evil

Although evil is not a creation of God, it is not simply a misperception or an illusion. While evil may not be real in the sense that it is not eternal, it does exist. The separation consciousness is a self-induced illusion, a misperception held by the soul. While acting under this misperception, however, the soul can and does create evil. Those things humanity defines as evil and as sin can only occur when we think we are separate from the person or thing we are violating.

Indifference leads to apathy, which is the foundation upon which all sin is built. It creates an attitude of despair and denial that allows injustice to occur uncontested. The failure to take action to prevent evil or to right a wrong is just as destructive as the evil itself. The Great Teachers have taught us that we are our brother's keeper. We have a moral and spiritual obligation to prevent evil by creating good. It is in the arena of moral responsibility that we have the most frequent opportunities to make decisions that prevent evil and create good. Yet moral courage at times appears more rare than physical courage. You need only think of the many newspaper headlines that tell of terrible crimes committed while people watched and did nothing.

Specialness creates a dualistic mentality whereby one sees himself as more deserving than others. It creates an imbalance and a one-sided perspective that prevents a person from making a connection with another. The behaviors that result—arrogance, greed, addiction, envy, and resentment—have harmful effects not only for others but also for the person committing these acts. When we engage in such behavior, we pull further away from our fellow spiritual beings. By doing so we retard our own spiritual development by reinforcing the barrier that separates us from the rest of creation. This prevents us from growing spiritually into a unity consciousness where we may realize our full potential as co-creators with God.

Fear is the most potent of all negative emotions. Since it is the direct misapplication of love, it can be as powerful, in a negative way, as the force of love is powerful in a positive way. Most people are familiar with the way physical fear can cripple our ability to react in dangerous situations; hence we have the expression "paralyzed with fear." Fear cripples us in the same way spiritually. Fear paralyzes our spiritual vision. It prevents us from seeing the truth of who and what we are and from knowing our true relationship to others and to God. Fear and the hate we feel when fearful stand in stark opposition to the loving power of God. Those who choose to remain in fear truly live in the darkness of evil forces.

Evil is real. It is the misuse of the creative abilities of the soul, the misapplication of creative energy. This force, this power, this energy, brought the universe into being. It created the elements, the worlds, and the stars. It created time and space. It created life in all its varied forms and expressions. When used incorrectly this power is equal in its destructive effects. The misapplication of creative energy can undo creation itself.

One reading indicates that disobedience on earth reflects upward to the heavenly hosts and influences the activities of God's command. (5757-1) Reading 815-3 tells us,

> "MAN in his madness, or in his selfishness, TURNS same [author's note: *spiritual power*] into that which becomes either as miracles in the experiences of man or crimes that make for the crying out of the people who heed not."

We must therefore be on guard against the complacency that comes from underestimating the power and reality of evil. In order to overcome evil, we must understand that evil is real and recognize that it is very powerful indeed.

9
The Function of Evil

I am part of that force which would do evil,
yet forever works the good.
Mephistopheles in <u>Faust</u>

We know from our studies thus far that God did not create evil. Souls rebelled against the Creative Force and brought evil into being. God, however, would not negate evil because that would be a violation of free will. We also know that after souls chose to believe in a separation consciousness while in spirit, God created the material dimension to give us the opportunity to realize the separation we had created. Given this fact, might it not be possible that after we had again erred, this time in the material world, God found a way to use the chaos and destruction that resulted from our choices as a means to create good? Let us therefore consider the idea that rather than condemn us for our errors of perception, God was able to use the evil we created in a positive way.

To explore this idea, we turn to a review of the monistic view of evil,[30] which states that God allows evil to exist because it serves some purpose in the divine plan. The monistic conception of evil might be considered a philosophy based upon the divine perspective rather than an egocentric viewpoint. From the egocentric view it appears there is a dualistic system at work, with Satan trying to thwart the purposes of God (good) whenever possible. From the divine perspective there is only one divine plan in which God allows evil to operate because it plays some essential, although not always understood, role.

Initially, this view of evil is difficult to understand. Yet it is only difficult to accept if we believe God created evil. While God will not violate our free will, He does not desire that we remain separated from Him. Rather than condemn us for our errors, He devised a way to use the evil we created for a higher purpose of good.

The Monistic View of Evil

One of the first Christian theologians to propose a monistic view of evil was Origen, who argued that Satan and/or evil are allowed to exist for God's own purposes. Origen taught that all of creation was working toward perfection, and that when all had reached this level, Satan would be saved and evil would cease to exist. Satan and evil, therefore, will eventually be won over to the side of good. St. Augustine proposed a similar doctrine, called *privatio boni*, which states that evil has no substance of its own but exists only as a diminishment of the good. John Calvin also accepted this view, believing that Satan was a creation of God and therefore subject to His will.

The idea that Satan acts as an agent of God and in some unknown way carries out his part in God's grand design has a scriptural basis. You may recall from Chapter Four that the Book of Job portrays Satan as an agent of God. In the Pseudepigraphic Book of Jubilees, the Mastema-Satan character has a role to play in the moral development of humanity. [31]

John A. Sanford, a modern Episcopalian theologian and Jungian analyst, points out that the monistic view of evil most accurately reflects Jesus' viewpoint as related in the Gospels of the New Testament. He states that despite the important role Satan plays in the New Testament, there is very little said about his origin or ultimate fate. There is also no explanation for his presence or for the presence of evil in the world. Jesus seemed to regard both Satan and evil as an inevitable part of creation. Sanford refers to the three following

Biblical passages as the best summation of Jesus'
attitude toward evil.

> "But I say to you, Love your enemies and
> pray for those who persecute you, so that
> you may be sons of your Father who is in
> heaven; for he makes his sun rise on the
> evil and on the good, and sends rain on
> the just and on the unjust." (Matthew
> 5:44-45)

> "Whoever receives one such child in my
> name receives me; but whoever causes one
> of these little ones who believes in me to
> sin *[author's note: from the Greek
> 'skandolon' meaning stumbling block, or
> to cause to stumble]*, it would be better for
> him to have a great millstone fastened
> round his neck and to be drowned in the
> depth of the sea. 'Woe to the world for
> temptations to sin! For it is necessary that
> temptations *[author's note: same Greek
> root word 'skandolon']* come, but woe to
> the man by whom the temptation comes!'"
> (Matthew 18:5-7)

> "I put it to you: is it against the law on the
> Sabbath to do good, or to do evil; to save life
> or to destroy it?" (Luke 6:10)

In the first passage from Matthew, we have Jesus
telling us that both the good and the evil receive the sun
and the rain. God treats both equally and makes no
attempt to eliminate evil in the world. In the second
passage from Matthew, Jesus speaks of the relationship of
children to the kingdom of heaven and addresses the
issue of those who bring evil into the experience of others.

He clearly says that stumbling blocks—evil—are necessary, but he does not explain why this so. He is also clear that those who become an instrument of evil will face dire consequences. In Luke, Jesus shows us that he believed it is fully within man's choice to decide whether he will be an instrument of good or an instrument of evil.

Sanford also stated that Jesus did not perform his ministry as an attempt to eliminate evil, but rather as a part of a divine plan that relates to the development of consciousness and the fulfillment of the personality. He makes a case that in all of Jesus' teachings, and in the events of the crucifixion and the resurrection, the emphasis is not upon evil as such but upon the development of the individual and his relationship to God. Once that is accomplished, the problem of evil takes care of itself.

The Process of Individuation

Variations on the monistic view of evil have been proposed by a number of theologians and philosophers, all of who believe in the necessity of evil in a morally meaningful world. They point to the necessity of polar opposites that allow us to distinguish and appreciate one state of existence from another. For example, how can we recognize the light without the darkness? How can we appreciate beauty without the ugliness? How can we have justice without injustice? How can we appreciate freedom without the threat of it being taken from us? How can we recognize truth if we cannot distinguish it from falsehood?

The monistic view of evil closely parallels what psychologists call the process of "individuation," a term first coined by the Swiss psychoanalyst Carl Jung. Jung proposed that the deepest instinct within any creature is to fulfill itself. In humans, this urge toward fulfillment comes from the unconscious mind and requires the forging of the conscious and unconscious minds acting in unison with each other. Jung called this lifelong process individuation, "the possibility, ingrained in the human species and present in everyone, whereby the individual psyche can attain its full development and completion."[32]

This process requires a person to confront her "shadow" self, "the thing a person has no wish to be."[33] The shadow self is defined as "a repository in the unconscious of all the things one cannot accept about oneself."[34] It is the sum of a person's unpleasant qualities including the inferior and primitive side of our nature. It is the dark side of one's personality. These aspects of personality normally lay dormant in the unconscious.

The goal of individuation is an indivisible, unified personality. In order for individuation to occur, the personality must become aware of its totality, including aspects of its shadow self. Few people, however, explore this part of themselves without a catalyst of some kind. For many, this catalyst is evil—pain, loss, or something that is destructive in some way. It is only when prompted by a power that seems to oppose wholeness that people find the wholeness within themselves.

From this psychoanalytic viewpoint, the existence of evil in the world plays a vital role in humanity's psychological development, since evil is necessary if individuation is to occur. Sanford expresses it this way,

> "...can there be soul-building, the building up of consciousness, moral fibre, and strengthened personalities, without dark-ness, sin, and destructiveness at work in the world for souls to work against?"[35]

Those who ascribe to this view believe that human beings must encounter resistance in order to reach their full potential. Just as steel grows strong through tempering, and broken bones that heal are stronger than before, so do humans grow strong by encountering, confronting, and overcoming adversity.

As you can see, the process of individuation parallels the monistic view of evil. The concept of spiritual development as described in the Edgar Cayce readings also presents a similar view.

Spiritual Development

The readings tell us that a soul enters the earth plane for the experience of learning lessons necessary for spiritual development and to have the opportunity to put spiritual truth into practice. Spiritual development is a long process. It is only after we have mastered one lesson and then **applied** that lesson in life that we are allowed to continue on to the next step. God is patient and merciful. We are given opportunity after opportunity to become the creative beings we were meant to be.

> "Not that man is awakened all at once, but here a little, there a little, line upon line, precept upon precept. Then as these are applied, as these become a part of the experience of the soul, there becomes the desire of the soul to find its rest, its peace, its hope in Him who is the Author of faith, of hope, of mercy, of love. Thus does the awareness come as to the purposes of man's advent into what we know as materiality." (262-119)

The readings state that very few experiences in our lives happen by chance. "Hence in the relationships, the meetings with others in WHATEVER form or manner, such are not coincidental but are rather as purposeful experiences." (1722-1) Every person we meet, each condition we encounter, and all the situations we face present us with an opportunity to learn lessons designed to bring us closer to a state of unity consciousness with God.

Many esoteric traditions teach that prior to entering the earth plane each soul is given the opportunity to **choose** what lessons it desires to learn. The soul is given the opportunity to see all the possibilities it may meet based upon the choices it makes. The soul rejects some, and agrees to others, accepting the possibilities and knowing that some may involve physical pain, emotional sorrow, or suffering. While in the spiritual realm, however, the soul sees the greater purpose that each experience may bring. The soul realizes that physical experiences are temporal and cannot truly harm it. The soul accepts those experiences in the knowledge that they will bring it closer to a state of unity consciousness with God.

When we enter the earth plane, however, "the veil" of this material world clouds our memory, and the reasons for which we came move into the subconscious level of our mind. We begin to see with our physical eyes rather than our spiritual vision. A good example of this is found in the Biblical story of the man, blind from birth, who came to Jesus seeking the restoration of his sight. Jesus' disciples asked him if the man's blindness was due to his sins or the sins of his parents. (Note that this question implies the disciples' belief in both karma and reincarnation because being born blind, the man's sins had to occur prior to his birth.) Jesus' response surprised them as He said that the man's blindness was due to neither. It had occurred so that the glory of God might be demonstrated through the man's healing.

The disciples were looking at the situation with their physical eyes while Jesus was looking with spiritual vision. He understood that this soul had accepted blindness as a condition of his life on earth so that Jesus could restore his sight and in so doing, perform a miracle. The story of that miracle has been told for two thousand years. Imagine how many souls have been touched and inspired by that soul's decision to endure blindness during that lifetime.

It is therefore possible that a soul will agree to endure what appear to be hurtful relationships and tragic conditions during a physical lifetime on earth. The most common reasons for doing so appear to be to learn a lesson, to teach others, or to make manifest the glory of God. In fact, the readings give numerous instances of "advanced" souls who entered the earth plane with a physical or mental disability or endured circumstances that caused great suffering so that others might learn from their associations with them. While the conscious mind of the person may not be aware of the choice made by the soul, the individual subconsciously knows and understands the reasons for the condition. The individual is also aware, on the soul level, that this condition is temporary in nature, and therefore is not something that can harm its true spiritual self.

A parallel can be drawn between the process of individuation and Cayce's concept of spiritual development. In individuation, the strongest desire of any human being is to fulfill its full potential. In the readings, this equates to the soul seeking to correct its errors of perception and realize its true nature and relationship with God. In individuation, this urge comes from the unconscious mind and requires the forging of the conscious and unconscious. The readings attribute this urge to "memory of First Cause," contained within the spirit (spark of God) of each human being. It is First Cause that prompts us to look beyond our five physical senses and integrate all three interrelated components of ourselves—body, mind, and soul. The goal of individuation is an indivisible, unified personality. The goal of spiritual development is a fully-integrated or "multisensory" human.[36]

The multisensory human is able to move beyond the perception of the five physical senses and perceive phenomena that exist in the world of pure spirit or energy. This enables the person to see with a new type of "spiritual" vision, look beyond old paradigms built upon differences (separation), and act according to paradigms based upon unity or God-consciousness. Simply put, the multisensory human becomes aware of his spiritual nature, and begins to act upon spiritual impulses rather than selfish desires.

In order for the process of individuation to succeed, a person must confront her shadow self. In order to awaken spiritually, a person must confront her true nature as a co-creator with God and acknowledge the fact that as creative beings, our thoughts and actions create our experience. While at first look this may not seem to equate to the "dark side" of the shadow self, it truly does equate, because this requires us to accept the fact that we create the evil as well as the good.

> "Ideas may be merely thoughts. As they run the course through those activities and minds of individuals, they may become crimes or they become miracles, dependent upon that with which the individual entity gives the thought or the idea to an ideal..." (5250-1)

The catalyst for individuation is something that is destructive or life-threatening to the individual, something we normally think of as evil. The catalyst for spiritual awakening is often adversity of some kind. The readings call these experiences stumbling blocks and frequently admonish us to take the stumbling blocks we encounter in our lives and turn them into stepping-stones toward greater growth and development. The story of Job is an excellent illustration of this process.

Job's Story

The Book of Job has historically been interpreted as an attempt to address the existence of evil and explain why good people suffer unjustly. Orthodox interpretations of Job, however, agree that the book does not present a clear-cut answer as to why innocents suffer. The reason for Job's misfortunes is never given to him. Instead, God's answer to Job is that the limitations of human wisdom prevent him from true understanding. I question whether this is really the moral of the lament of Job. Surely this Scripture must be more than a story to teach us that the limited human condition can never understand the workings of divine power.

The Book of Job tells us that he was a righteous man and that none of the misfortunes that befell him were due to his own making. If you accept the premise that the soul chooses the lessons it desires to work on while in the physical plane, you accept that Job **chose** the experiences he encountered, knowing the great soul growth that would occur if he met those experiences with the right spirit.

Scripture clearly indicates that Job met the many misfortunes of his later life in the same spirit he had met the good fortune of his early life—with patience, understanding, and faith. When faced with the loss of his livestock and the death of his servants and children, Job steadfastly continued to praise and worship God. When afflicted with a debilitating disease he refused to heed his wife's advice and curse God.

Job could easily have reacted with anger and even hatred toward God for all the evil that befell him. Some might even say that he was justified in doing so. If he had made that choice, however, he would have separated himself from God and fostered a separation consciousness. Instead, in each instance Job chose to manifest the spiritual attributes of good and thereby reaffirm a unity consciousness between himself and his Creator. Because of the misfortunes he experienced, Job saw and knew both good and evil, and through free will, made the choice to manifest good. By returning good for evil, Job experienced a high level of spiritual growth. Not in spite of, but **because** of his experiences, Job became closer to God than he had been before.

Turning Evil to Good

Many different schools of thought teach us that it is the difficult things in life—the trials, temptations, stumbling blocks, adversity, and evil—which, if met with the right attitude, serve as an impetus to greater growth and wholeness. From a psychological perspective, the opportunity to encounter adversity and overcome it enables us to tap into portions of our psyche that help us become whole and fully functioning individuals capable of meeting our true potential.

From a spiritual perspective, the challenges we meet in life enable us to reach a higher level of spiritual growth. The Book of Job certainly carries this message. Jesus said that temptations (stumbling blocks) must come as a necessary experience in life. The Buddha expressed this sentiment when he said that it is our enemy who teaches us the most valuable lessons. The Edgar Cayce readings teach us that such things present sent us with opportunities and lessons designed to further our spiritual development toward a closer oneness with God.

The process whereby we learn to grow through adversity is a separate study in itself and far beyond the scope of this book. There are many excellent books that deal with this issue, both from a psychological viewpoint and a spiritual perspective. The focus of these studies is on teaching people to respond in a positive rather than a negative way, whether it be having the right attitude, seeing adversity as a means to create positive change, or practicing spiritual ideals such as compassion, forgiveness, and love. Those desiring further information on these processes are advised to consult the "self-help" section of any bookstore or library.

It would seem as if evil does indeed serve a positive function in our spiritual development in that it requires us to make choices by which we learn to use our will in accordance Divine Will. We need to remember, however, that God did not intend for evil to be a necessary part of our spiritual development. Rather, our choices in defiance of Divine Will led us to this situation.

It is not evil in itself that serves a positive function in our spiritual development. Rather, it is our **response** to evil that will either help us or hinder us in our spiritual growth.

If we respond to evil from the limited egocentric viewpoint, we return evil for evil and loose an opportunity for spiritual growth. If we respond to evil from a divine perspective, we make a choice to rise above surface appearances and search for the lesson each experience presents. We demonstrate our belief that there is a higher order and wisdom at work in the world. We move beyond a separation consciousness based on appearances and reaffirm our unity with God. By facing the difficult things that evil brings our way, and through the divine perspective responding appropriately, we also take action against evil by using it as an opportunity to create good.

10
Synthesis

We were born to create, and we always have the choice
of whether we will create for good or for evil.
And the wondrous thing is that with every new moment
we have the opportunity of choosing again.
Rosemary Fillmore Rhea, "A New Heaven and New Earth,"
New Thought for a New Millennium

In the preceding chapters, we have explored the many dimensions of good and evil from both a traditional viewpoint as well as the metaphysical perspective of the Edgar Cayce readings. We have discussed the complexities of the what, how, and why of good and evil from a material, mental, and spiritual viewpoint. By doing this, I believe we have come to a better understanding of good and evil from a divine perspective and overcome problems associated with a more limited, egocentric view. During this process we also discovered more about ourselves, who we are, why we were created, and our place in the universe. Let us take a moment to summarize what we have learned.

On a spiritual level, good is the awareness of one's true spiritual nature and relationship to God. It is unity consciousness with the Creative Force. Since it is a direct expression of the Creative Force, good exists as an eternal aspect of creation. On a mental or archetypal level, good is characterized by the following qualities: order, light, spirit, spiritual truth, reason, law, and Divine Will. In the physical world, good can be defined as life-promoting behaviors that value the greater good over self-interest. Life-promoting behaviors unite people rather than separate them.

From a spiritual perspective, evil is the lack of awareness of one's true spiritual self and the self's relation to God. It is a separation consciousness. While evil is not real in the sense that it is not an original creation and therefore not eternal, the influence and power of evil is very real. On the mental or archetypal level, evil embodies the following qualities: chaos, darkness, physical being, ignorance, falsehood, desire, rebellion, and selfishness. On the material plane a separation consciousness leads to three life perspectives—indifference, dualism, and fear. These perspectives cause a person to act out life-threatening behaviors that advance the self-interests of an individual or a group over the interests of the human community. These life-threatening behaviors, also called sin, divide and separate.

The soul was created when God, as Spirit, extended itself and brought individualized expressions of itself into being. God intended that we be co-creators and companions. To be truly "as God," the soul was given free will so that it might freely express itself. Through the will, we can apply our creative abilities in accordance with spiritual ideals or we can defy Divine Will and create chaos and destruction.

While in spiritual form, the existence of evil as a state of separation from the Creative Force made it possible for the soul to experience different levels of consciousness. For only by knowing all levels of existence and through free will choosing its path could the soul truly be a companion with God rather than a servant. However, the choice by the soul to accept this perception as reality brought evil into existence in the spiritual dimension.

God then brought the material dimension into being so that the contrast between good and evil in the earth plane might enable us to clearly see the difference between separation from the Creative Force and unity with it. Once on earth, the soul again erred in perception, believing itself to be the source of creative power rather than a channel through which it flowed. By misapplying its creative abilities in defiance of divine and natural law, the soul brought evil into the material world.

Despite our continued erroneous choices, however, God decided that the evil we created serve a positive function. Our experiences with evil provide us with an opportunity to clearly see the difference between good and evil, God and "not God," so we can make choices that lead us to a higher level of spiritual development. The choices we make affect not only us; they also impact the future of humankind.

The final step in our study is to take the ideas presented thus far and use them as a guide to help us make the right choices and take the right action to oppose evil and overcome it. Based on what we have learned, the first step in opposing evil is to be diligent against it. The next step is to respond to evil with right action in the right spirit. If we do not respond to evil in the right spirit, we not only perpetrate evil but we also lose the opportunity to create good. The third step necessary to overcome evil is to use every moment as an opportunity to create good.

Diligence Against Evil

The secularization of thought that occurred in recent generations caused us to lose our diligence against evil. By focusing on secular concerns we distanced ourselves from evil and ignored the reality of its destructive power. It is as if we looked at the world with blinders on, often thinking evil was nothing more than ignorance or even an illusion. The well-known Jewish theologian Martin Buber warned against this self-imposed blindness when he said, "Man knows of the chaos and creation in the cosmogenic myth and he learns that chaos and creation take place in himself, but he does not see the former and latter together."[37]

Being diligent against evil means we must accept the fact that people do create evil. Some choose to do so out of hate; they act strictly out of malice. Others make choices based on false perceptions and mis-interpretations. Included here are religious zealots who believe they are carrying out the work of God by killing those who hold different beliefs. Whether a person chooses to enact evil out of malice or makes this choice based on a misguided perception is irrelevant. Their actions create the same chaos and destruction and further divide us.

Diligence against evil also requires that we respect the influence and power of evil and acknowledge that it can cause great harm to those against which it is directed. I believe that the events of September 11, 2001 reminded us of the power of evil in a most painful and horrific way. The death and destruction we saw that day served as a wake up call, a reminder that evil is real and can strike anyone, anytime, anywhere. Since that day many people are coming to the realization that we cannot afford to ignore the destructive power of evil.

Being diligent against evil also compels us to recognize that evil is our creation. It originates in the human heart, mind, and soul. By denying this and seeing evil as something outside ourselves, we distance ourselves from evil. By distancing ourselves from evil, we more easily fall prey to its influence. The noted psychologist Eric Fromm warned against this danger with these words, "As long as one believes that the evil man wears horns, one will not discover an evil man."[38]

Diligence against evil does not mean we should fear evil. Evil is our creation; it only has the power we give it. Evil is not an independent principle that exists apart from good. It is not a cosmic force that exists outside of us and seeks to control us. There is no all-powerful being that pulls us into the fiery pits of hell. We choose to create evil. We can make another choice as well.

Right Action

One choice that we all must make is how to respond to the evil that occurs in our lives. When faced with evil we can respond in one of two ways. We can respond in kind and return evil for evil or we can respond to evil with good. Responding to evil with good can take one of two forms: nonviolent nonresistance as practiced by Buddha, Jesus of Nazareth, and other Great Teachers, and nonviolent resistance as demonstrated by Mahatma Ghandi and Martin Luther King, Jr. Returning evil for evil usually takes the form of violent resistance and can include retaliation, armed conflict, and war.

In *The Seat of the Soul*, Gary Zukav equates evil with darkness and makes the point that evil should be understood for what it really is—the dynamic of the absence of light, light being equated with Divine Intelligence or God.[39] Zukav argues that since evil is an absence you must counter it with a presence. If you take a burned-out lantern into a dark room, the darkness continues. If you take a candle into a dark room, however, the light immediately displaces the darkness.

If you hate in response to evil, all you have is a double helping of hate. You increase evil rather than diminish it. If evil is the absence of God, you can only overcome evil by bringing God—love—to it. When you bring love to any situation, you bring the creative power of the universe into action. We triumph over evil not by resisting it, but by replacing it with love.

Throughout history the Great Teachers have taught that this way, the way of nonviolent nonresistance, holds the key to spiritual enlightenment. Buddha, Jesus of Nazareth and many other religious teachers urge us to adopt a divine perspective and respond to those who commit evil with compassion, forgiveness, and love. We are to do so in the hope that those who commit evil will see that there is another way.

Adopting the divine perspective does not mean we should allow evil to continue or hatred to endure. To the contrary, we have a moral and spiritual obligation to oppose evil wherever and whenever we find it. If we do not oppose evil, we become co-creators of evil, for our indifference and inaction allow evil to exist.

It is an unfortunate fact that there are still those in this world who are so blinded by fear and hatred that they cannot see another way. They will take every opportunity available to create evil. Fear is a very powerful motivator and as we noted earlier it is the root of all hatred. Much of the evil we see today is committed by people who fear and hate those they perceive as different. Others promote their own self-interests in defiance of the greater community good. Still others act out of the deluded perception they are carrying out the Divine Will of God. These misguided souls will not respond in kind to compassion and love. When confronted with the evil they create, we must do as Martin Buber advised and take right action to "deprive evil of its power." We must take right action against evil on both the individual and national level.

There is a basic difference between an individual response to evil and a response from a group or nation. A nation will rarely if ever respond with nonviolent nonresistance, particularly when confronted with evil that threatens its very existence. Nonviolent resistance, such as we saw during the call to Indian nationalism and the Civil Rights movement in the United States, is also rare. It has only been successfully applied against an institutionalized type of political evil.

When threatened with evil, nations most often react with violent resistance, which includes armed conflict and war. Yet even nations that take armed action against evil can do so from a divine perspective. The key here is to take **right action** against evil to prevent its continuation while responding in the **right spirit**.

Responding in the right spirit means that we cannot allow our actions to be motivated by negative emotions such as revenge, anger, and hate. We must gauge our response to effectively eliminate future threats and yet not allow ourselves to be overcome by our own negative emotions.

There is much truth in Mahatma Ghandi's observation that the old "eye for an eye" mentality would leave the whole world sightless. When we respond to evil from the limited egocentric viewpoint, we return evil for evil and continue the cycle of violence and hate. By holding to the highest spiritual ideal when responding to evil, we take only what action is necessary to prevent the continuation of evil. We cease to create more evil and take the first step in breaking the cycle of hatred and violence that has long plagued humanity. Further, by facing evil from the divine perspective and responding in the right spirit, we take action against evil by using it as an opportunity to create good.

Creating Good

The idea that we choose to create good or evil is reflected in many of the teachings we have already reviewed. Mana, the life force that exists in all creation, was neither good nor evil. It derived its character from the intentions of the person channeling its power. In the teachings of the Tao, adherence to the "way of Tao" is a choice a person makes. Plato saw good and evil as a choice between Reason and Necessity. A similar idea is also found in Stoic philosophy.

Zoroaster taught that life on earth was a continual struggle between the forces of good and the forces of evil. In the Jewish tradition, evil occurs in response to human choices that are contrary to the will of God. This idea carried over into Christianity with the idea of moral good and evil. Moral evil was the willful deprivation of good that occurred when God's creations chose to reject their true natures and sought to be something they were not. Moral evil entered the material world through the actions of Adam and Eve who made the choice to eat the fruit of the Tree of Knowledge despite God's warning not to do so.

Even the scientific community stands in agreement on this issue. Science tells us that humans possess the capacity for both good and evil. The consensus is that the demonstration of good or evil behavior depends upon a complex combination of hereditary factors, environmental conditions, and individual choice.

The readings also tell us that what we choose to create is determined by the ideal to which our mind is attuned. As Reading 1011-1 explains, we create good or evil according to the ideal we hold.

> "...this entity (as others) comes to make more manifested the consciousness or awareness of those influences for good and evil in the experience of the soul; and through the application of that set as the ideal grow towards a unison with that ideal. Each individual entity, whether aware of same or not, sets before self an ideal in the material world, in the mental world, in the spiritual world."

When we hold an ideal that is based in the material world, materialism becomes the center of our focus. We interact with the world through our conscious mind, evaluate our experiences through the five physical senses, and see ourselves as physical beings separate from others. When we do this, we create from a separation consciousness. Our thoughts emphasize the differences between us, emotions flow from fear and we put self-interest above the greater good of the human community. As a result our actions are characterized by behavior that is life-threatening and destructive.

When we hold to a spiritual ideal, however, we acknowledge our true nature as spiritual beings. We evaluate our experiences from a divine perspective and apply our creative abilities from a state of unity consciousness. As multisensory humans who acknowledge body, mind, and soul, our thoughts emphasize the oneness of all creation, our emotions are based in love, and the highest good of humanity as a whole becomes our goal. Our actions are life-promoting behaviors that advance our own spiritual growth as we help others.

The simple fact is that we have a choice as to what we will create. We can choose to create good or we can choose to create evil. Reading 2549-1 expresses this as follows.

> "For, know that each soul is a free-willed individual, and chooses the way and the application. For it is either the co-worker with God in creation - and creative then in its attitude, in its thought, in its application of tenets and truths day by day; OR in attune with that which is at variance, and thus besetting or putting stumbling blocks in the way of others along the way. Each soul must choose of itself whom it will serve..."

A Lesson From the Past

As we learned in Chapter Seven, there has been a continual conflict between those souls that choose to create good and those that choose to create evil. This war is cosmic in nature and has been ongoing since Satan first made the choice to believe the erroneous thought of separation was real. The turmoil we see on earth is only a reflection of the warring between the forces of light and the forces of darkness in the spiritual dimension. The many forms this war has taken on earth can be found in any history book.

The Edgar Cayce readings, however, contain an interesting story that provides us with an account of how this cosmic war first manifested on earth. I relate this story, the story of Atlantis,[40] for two reasons. First, the themes it presents are familiar ones and provide the blueprint for the way this war has repeatedly played out on earth. Second, although the story takes place thousands of years ago in the long-forgotten past, it does not end there. For the story of Atlantis also contains a warning for us at this critical time in history.

The readings tell us that philosophical differences led to a division of the Atlanteans into two opposing factions: the Children of the Law of One and the Sons of Belial.[41] In an attempt to use less gender-specific terms, I have chosen to call these groups the Keepers of the Law of One and the Followers of Belial, respectively.

Both groups entered into the material body to manifest their creative spiritual abilities in the material world. The Keepers of the Law of One exercised these creative abilities in accordance with Divine Will. The Followers of Belial rejected this premise. They were "Those individuals who had through their sojourns in the earth as souls pushed into matter as to become separate entities, without the consideration of principle or the ability of self-control." (2464-2) They focused on the physical attributes of the body and began to "use spiritual forces for the satisfying of material appetites." (2850-1) They had no consideration for the hardships their activities caused others.

There was also a third group in existence at this time, which the readings call "automatons." They appear to have been less evolved than the Atlanteans, physically and mentally. They were servants and laborers, and "were considered by many as merely THINGS rather than individual souls." (1744-1) This third group appears to have been the result of an evolutionary "mistake" and included the descendants of those who had projected themselves into matter in a manner contrary to natural and spiritual law.

The initial antagonism between the Keepers of the Law of One and the Followers of Belial centered on the treatment of the laborers. The Followers of Belial wanted to keep the status quo, believing that the laborers existed solely to serve their needs. The Followers of the Law of One wanted to improve conditions for these less advanced individuals. As Reading 2464-2 tells us, "...there were those disputations with them as to the purposes of the children of Belial; that these were to be exploited rather than to be made equals with those thus endowed with the spiritual understanding." The following two readings give us an interesting and personal insight into this debate.

> "...the entity was the timekeeper for those who were called things, or the servants, or the workers of the peoples and the entity felt latent and manifest, as in the present, the wanting to reform, to change things, so that every individual soul had the right to freedom of speech, freedom of thought, freedom of activity...And the entity saw, the entity felt the need of God's hand in what evil, or Satan, had brought in the earth." (5249-1)

> "...when there were the wagings of the eternal laws of the One with those that worshiped Belial, those that worshipped

> the satisfying of physical desire, those that
> worshipped ease and pleasure in the
> material world. The entity then was
> among the priests of the law of One, that
> pitted self against many of those things
> that were presented by a people that were
> being drawn gradually into self-
> indulgences." (640-1)

The division between the two groups intensified over time. The Followers of Belial increased their efforts to use spiritual power for self-gratification and material gain. They eventually sought domination not only over other beings but also over the laws of nature itself. The misuse of their creative abilities in attempts to control the forces of nature resulted in catastrophic consequences as noted in the reading below.

> "Before that we find the entity was in that
> land now known...as the Atlantean,
> during those days when there were the
> attempts of those to bring quiet, to bring
> order out of chaos by the destructive
> forces that had made for the eruptions in
> the land that had divided the lands and
> had changed not only the temperate but
> to a more torrid region by the shifting of
> the activities of the earth itself." (884-1)

While their intent was not to destroy the land, their misguided attempts to harness certain forces of nature resulted in three separate "upheavals." The first upheaval divided the continent of Atlantis into five islands. "Before that we find the entity was in the Atlantean experience when there was the breaking up of the land itself through the use of SPIRITUAL truths for the material gains of physical power." (1152-1)

The second upheaval resulted in the sinking of two of the five islands. "Before that we find the entity was in the Atlantean land, when there were those periods just after the second of the breaking-ups of the land owing to the misapplications of divine laws upon those things of nature or of earth...."(1298-1)

Despite these disasters, the Followers of Belial continued on the same path and the friction between the two groups grew.   Consider excerpts from the following two readings:

> "Before that we find the entity was in the Atlantean land, when there were those periods of disturbances owing to those confusions arising between those in authority that would make for the universality of knowledge of all natures and those that held for castes and for positions." (1302-2)

> "Before that we find the entity was in the Atlantean land, during those periods when there were those activities that brought about the last destruction of same through the warrings between the children of the Law of One and the sons of Belial or Bel (?). [Baal] There the entity was among those who waned between the children of faith or the Law of One and those who sought the use of the spiritual forces for their own self-indulgences, self-aggrandizements." (1599-1)

Clearly the Followers of Belial did not learn from their previous mistakes. Nor did the Keepers of the Law of One take strong enough action to oppose them. By the time anyone realized the extent of the situation, it was too late to stop the destructive forces that had been unleashed. Atlantis was destroyed. The readings indicate that with what little time they had left, a number of Atlanteans escaped to "safety lands" where stories of their homeland became the basis of myths and legends.

A Warning for Today

Whether you accept the story of Atlantis as truth or fiction, you can see that it contains all the elements of the classic story of good versus evil, a story that has been repeated all too often during the course of recorded history. Of more importance, however, is the warning inherent in this tale, for the readings draw a parallel between the world of Atlantis and the world today. They tell us the soul groups that played a part in the Atlantean story are returning to the earth plane in ever increasing numbers, particularly since the early Twentieth Century. More significant is the fact that many of these souls have the potential to greatly influence world events as they are coming back to positions of power and authority.

> "For, it is not by chance that any soul enters a particular period. As indicated in this entity here, it is an Atlantean. Hence it is manifesting in the earth at a period when many Atlanteans have entered. For, ye may be very sure, there is not a leader in any country or any clime, whether friend or foe of what this entity thinks, that was not an Atlantean." (2794-3)

Some of those returning have no doubt learned a great deal since they followed the ways of Belial. We can only hope that they are coming back with the intention to "do it right" this time. Others may have learned very little during their intervening experiences and are returning with the same misguided beliefs. Still others may have returned with a renewed purpose, determined not to let their inaction allow a similar disaster to occur again. There may also be those who, having made the right decisions in Atlantis, will find this life's temptations too great to bear and make the wrong choices. All intend to complete the drama begun so long ago, returning to earth at time when humanity possesses the technological ability to destroy itself.

It is our technology, perhaps, that makes this the most critical time we have ever faced in history. Matthew Fox makes the point that, "evil abounds when humanity's capacity for creativity is the greatest."[42] It was the high level of technology we now possess that enabled the terrorist attacks of September 11, 2001, to have such devastating effects. As our level of technological development increases so does our capacity for perpetrating evil upon others. Technology raises the battle between good and evil to a whole new level of destruction.

We have already seen the beginnings of this escalated battle in the world wars of the last century. We have witnessed its horror in the Holocaust and in ethnic cleansing campaigns from Cambodia to Africa to southern Europe. We have seen its innocent victims in the faces of children in Ireland, Bosnia, and the Middle East. We have felt its hatred in the terrorist attacks on our own country.

This type of evil is overt evil, a violent evil that is clearly evident to all. The Atlantean saga also warns us of another type of evil, a more subtle and more dangerous form of evil. It is an evil that comes from within our own house. It is the evil that occurs when those in power sponsor programs and policies that favor special interest groups over the common citizen. It is the evil that occurs when governments and private industry misuse the natural resources of this planet for monetary gain. It is the evil that occurs when a political party believes its own agenda is more righteous in the eyes of God than that of another.

This covert type of evil is easy to overlook, particularly when we are faced with the violence of life-threatening evil from outside sources. Yet it has the same disastrous consequences as any action based in a separation consciousness. While these actions may appear morally justified, they promote specialness and dualism and lead us down the same road as that taken by the Followers of Belial. This is why we must be especially diligent against the evil that can destroy us from within.

Prophecies from many traditions speak of this generation in history as a time when the forces of good will contend with the forces of evil on a scale never before witnessed by humanity. In the Christian tradition, this battle is known as Armageddon. Many believe that we are indeed standing on the brink of Armageddon. Yet despite the evil we see let loose in the world, there is still hope that we can and will find a better way.

Evil is our creation; we choose to create it. We can also make a choice to create in another way. The prophecies that speak of Armageddon also speak to this time as one of great opportunity when humanity can create a new world based on the spiritual principles of a unity consciousness. We do not have to repeat the mistakes of the past. We can rise above the limited five sensory perception of separation consciousness that has so long dominated human thought. We can choose to claim our birthright as companions and co-creators with God and "become who we are." We can make the choice to create good.

Hope for the Future

Yet even if we acknowledge the fact that we are creative beings, how do we, as individuals, make a difference? The answer is to create good wherever and whenever we can. The great religious traditions repeatedly teach us that the ordinary experiences of daily life provide opportunities to manifest thoughts and behaviors that will either hasten or retard our spiritual development. It is here in the little things that we can make a difference, not only in our own lives, but also in the lives of others and ultimately for the benefit of all humanity.

We are in a constant state of creation. Each thought we think, each word we say, and each action we take spirals outward and affects others. Each time a soul raises its own spiritual consciousness it raises the consciousness of humanity a little bit higher as well. Each experience we encounter, even those seemingly insignificant moments of ordinary life, presents us with a creative opportunity to become a catalyst for positive change.

Further, we need to know that we are not alone in our battle against evil. The spiritual forces of goodness and light stand ready to help us, particularly at this critical time in history. Consider Reading 3976-15:

> "And, as there is the wavering of those that would enter as emissaries, as teachers, from the throne of life, the throne of light, the throne of immortality, and *wage war in the air with those of darkness* [italics for author's emphasis], then know ye the Armageddon is at hand. For with the great numbers of the gathering of the hosts of those that have hindered and would make for man and his

weaknesses stumbling blocks, they shall *wage war with the spirits of light* [italics for author's emphasis] that come into the earth for this awakening...."

Angels guide and protect us. Archangels guard our way. There are also indications through psychic sources that for the first time in history, the Brotherhood of Masters will intervene on the **physical plane**. All the forces of goodness and light that exist in spirit stand ready to assist. We need only be open to this guidance and ask for their help.

In this generation we are awakening to the fact that we are spiritual beings endowed with creative abilities. We possess the capability to create our future and direct the course of our evolution. Given our profound powers of creativity, we have a serious responsibility to make those choices that will result in the highest good for all humankind. The choices we make will determine the course of history for generations to come. As we manifest a unity consciousness in our thoughts, words, and deeds, and make choices that reflect the attributes of good, we will create the best of all possible futures. As we do so, we fulfill our destiny as heirs and co-creators with God.

APPENDICES

Appendix A
Archetypes of Good and Evil

Good as Order; Evil as Chaos

The idea of associating good with order and evil with chaos may find its origin in creation mythology. Creation myths are stories that explain the origin of the world and how its inhabitants, animals and human, came into being. In creation myths, the world is brought into existence through the imposition of order upon a primeval state of existence. This primal state is often depicted as one of chaos, devoid of form and uninhabitable. The creative act occurs when a cosmic force acts to impose order upon the primal state. By this act, the chaotic state is transformed into a habitable world. Life is good and therefore the order that brings it into existence is good. Conversely, the primordial state of chaos is evil.

The initiator of order may be an impersonal principle, such as *wu* of Tao, Brahman of Buddhism, or the Logos of Stoicism. Order may also be imposed by a personal deity such as Plato's "demiurge," who brought forth order by impressing Forms upon matter. In Hinduism, Brahma is the creative aspect, responsible for creating the world at the beginning of each new cycle of existence. Vishnu, the Redeemer, is the preserver and protector of the world. Through his actions he brings order and discipline to humanity and is responsible for the reordering of the world following each cyclic creation. Shiva, the Destroyer, brings about the cyclic dissolution—chaos and destruction—of the world. Shiva is not portrayed as a purely evil god but is depicted in both terrible and graceful forms. This dual picture is due to the fact that in Hinduism, chaos possesses a transforming quality. While human perception initially views chaos as terrible and evil, the changes it brings can lead to a state of growth and enlightenment. The idea of chaos as transforming can be traced back to the Vedic tradition of Brahman where chaos is a different expression of the infinite whole.

In the Biblical story of Genesis, the God of Abraham brings creative order to the formless earth. "The earth was without form and void, and darkness was upon the face of the deep; and the Spirit of God was moving over the face of the waters. God said, 'Let there be light;' and there was light." (Genesis 1:2-3)

The Biblical account of Adam and Eve continues the good as order/evil as chaos analogy. By eating the forbidden fruit of the Tree of Knowledge, Adam and Eve turned creation upside down. Natural law was nullified, as man and woman were required to live in a manner different from that originally intended by God. They now had to create a life for themselves by toiling in a world that is harsh and uncaring. Because of their rejection of God's Divine Order, their idyllic existence in the Garden of Eden is replaced by confusion and unknowing as they venture forth into a chaotic new world.

This story is similar to that told in the Edgar Cayce readings:

> "...man – by HIS COMPLIANCE with divine law – bring[s] ORDER out of chaos; or, by his DISREGARD of the associations and laws of divine influence, bring[s] chaos and DESTRUCTIVE forces into his experience." (416-7)

The idea of order as good and disorder as evil exists in modern thought as well. Matthew Fox states, "Chaos happens when evil happens; it constitutes the undoing of creation."[43] It is evident in something as innocuous as our attitudes toward change. Modern studies have shown that any change, be it a new job, a move to a new location, divorce, the birth of a child, or death of a family member, creates stress in our lives. Even positive change such as childbirth or promotion to a more prestigious job causes stress. The reason for this is that order provides structure and therefore meaning to our lives. Order is good because it helps us define our existence and our place in the world. Any factor that reorders our world, even in a positive way, is initially perceived as disruptive. It is evil in the sense that it causes confusion and requires new patterns of behavior and response.

The correlation of evil with chaos becomes even clearer if we consider how we perceive evil. Actions considered evil are those that interfere with the established order of things. Theft, murder, and betrayal bring disruption to our lives on a personal level. Riots, terrorism, and war bring the same disruptive influence to the established order on a larger, sometimes global scale. It can be argued, therefore, that in the purest and most impersonal form, good is the principle of order and regulation while evil is the principle of chaos and disruption.

Good as Light; Evil as Darkness

The idea that light represents the power of good while darkness represents the forces of evil exists in all cultures. The sun-god concept common to the mythology of the ancient Egyptians, Babylonians, and Persians expressed this belief. So did the ancient Hebrew tradition. Continuing with the Biblical story of creation as noted above we see that "...God saw that the light was good; and God separated the light from the darkness." (Genesis 1:4) (Note that Genesis does not say that God created the darkness.) The good as light and evil as darkness dichotomy is also found in Hinduism and Zoroastrianism. Plato linked the Form of the Good with light, drawing a correlation between it and the physical sun. He believed that the Form of the Good is to the real world what the sun is to the physical world. Jesus taught, "For every one who does evil hates the light...But he who does what is true comes to the light...." (John 3:20-21)

As we learned in Chapter Ten, in *The Seat of the Soul*, Gary Zukav informs us that fiber optics proves white light is the integration of all the colors of the visible spectrum while black is the absence of that spectrum. He further equates light with energy, and Conscious Light with Divine Intelligence.[44]

This idea fits very well with a related corollary that associates light with knowledge and darkness with ignorance. In the *Republic*, Plato uses the analogy of a cave to illustrate this idea. He describes an image of human beings chained to the wall of a dark subterranean cave. They face the wall of the cave and are unable to move and see the light of a fire burning above and behind them. As something outside the cave passes in front of the light, it casts a shadow on the wall. Those who are chained see only the shadow and perceive it to be real. Someone who is freed from the chains, however, and moves outside the cave, can view the "real" object. Once outside the cave he understands that the shadow is only a projection of reality.

In this analogy, the shadows and darkness of the cave in which humanity is trapped are the chains of ignorance that hold us prisoner to the illusion created by our limited five senses. Knowledge of the real world is attained by breaking the chains of ignorance so we may move into the real world of the light of the Good. Knowledge, or the application of good, is therefore the remedy for ignorance or evil.

In religious writings, light is associated with spiritual consciousness while darkness refers to a lack of spiritual awareness. The Bible is filled with such examples, a few of which are given here. "...O that we might see some good! Lift up the light of thy countenance upon us, O Lord!" (Psalm 4:6) "Thy word is a lamp to my feet and a light to my path." (Psalm 119:105) "For it is the God who said, 'Let light shine out of darkness,' who has shone in our hearts to give the light of the knowledge of the glory of God in the face of Christ." (2 Corinthians 4:6) These are but a few of the many such analogies in the Bible.

The readings also provide excellent examples of this correlation. They equate light with spiritual knowledge of the oneness of all creation. Darkness refers to the rejection of that knowledge in favor of an erroneous perception of separation from God.

> "Hence these [light and darkness], then, are figures of that from the spiritual as facing the light and the dark, or facing the source of light - which, to the mind of those that seek to know His biddings, is the voice, the word, the life, the light that comes in the hearts, minds, souls of each to *awaken* [italics for author's emphasis] them, as individuals, to their relationships with the source of light." (262-55)

The universal identification of good with light and evil with darkness is likely due to the fact that the human species is diurnal, and most vulnerable to predators at night. Our sensory ability of sight enabled us to readily identify phenomena during daylight hours and that knowledge gave us a sense of security and power. As darkness fell, however, our sensory perception of the world was dulled so that we could not easily identify danger. We were ignorant of the outer world during the night and that ignorance made us feel vulnerable. Daylight was a time of productive activity that ensured our survival; hence its association with things that are known and good. The darkness of night, however, held unknown dangers. Hence its association with hidden dangers, or evil.

The Spirit Versus the Flesh

The third analogy originates in an association that linked good with things of the eternal, spiritual realm and evil with things of a temporal and physical nature. Attempts to understand the extremes of good and evil in human behavior led to the conclusion that we must possess a dual nature—we are both body and soul. Those things that pertained to the spiritual side of humankind were thought to be reflections of the divine good, while the drives and desires that came from our physical nature came to be seen as evil.

The belief that human beings are both spiritual and physical beings is found in most religious teachings. The Vendata teachings of the *Upanishads* teach the understanding of the individual self or soul (Atman) in relation to the universal essence or reality (Brahman). They emphasize the attainment of pure consciousness as the means of liberation from the physical world. The *Bhagavad-Gita*, the most sacred of all Hindu texts, addresses the dual nature of humanity by referring to a divine self within a material being. Hinduism associated the Atman or "breath" with the individual self, which is eternal and reborn into many physical existences.

The distinction between body and soul was a primary tenet of the religion of ancient Egypt, whose major beliefs stressed the immortality of the soul and resurrection of the body. *The Book of the Dead*, a compilation of over one hundred texts translated from Egyptian writings of the 18th and 19th Dynasties, provides explicit directions and rituals for aiding the dead and providing the soul with directions for its journey through the underworld and final judgment before the god Osiris.

Greek philosophers divided humans into two parts: the body, our physical self, and the psyche, which was preexistent and immortal. Zeno of Citium taught that the true essence of the soul was reason or logos. Plato called the body the prison house of the soul. In the *Phaedo* he portrays the life of the true philosopher as one in which the motives of the soul are separated from the body.

In the Judaic-Christian tradition, the Biblical book of Genesis details the creation of the soul and the physical body. The first chapter tells of our spiritual creation. "Then God said, 'Let us make man in our image, after our likeness'...So God created man in his own image, in the image of God he created him; male and female, he created them." (Genesis 1:26-27) The second chapter tells of the creation of the physical body and its animation by the soul force. "Then the Lord God formed man of dust from the ground, and breathed into his nostrils the breath of life; and man became a living being." (Genesis 2:7) Christian doctrine accepted the distinctness of body and soul, believing that humankind was a unique creation made in the image of God.

While most spiritual teachings did not view the body as inherently evil, they did accept that human passions, emotions, and desires should be eliminated. For example, while Taoism makes no intrinsic value judgments about good and evil, it does teach that good is achieved through the elimination of physical wants, desires, and aggression. The Noble Truths of Buddhism teach that the suffering which characterizes existence is caused by desire. Desire can be eliminated by following the Eightfold Path that traverses the Middle Way between the extremes of asceticism and earthly desires.

Plato associated good with reason and intellect and related evil to emotions and passion. His teachings had a direct impact upon Stoic philosophy and influenced Christianity in later centuries.

Nowhere is the good as spirit and evil as flesh analogy more pronounced than in the radical dichotomy found in Christian theology, due in large part to St. Paul. St. Paul made a radical distinction between the physical and the spiritual, using the word *sarx* when referring to the body. Sarx, however, actually means "flesh" rather than the body (*soma*). St. Paul used it to refer to man's unredeemed nature and mortal weakness that caused humans to be subject to the lower negative forces of evil.

His choice of the word flesh to represent the incarnate center of sin and evil, however, was to have lasting consequences for Christian thought, as future Christian theologians came to associate evil and sin with the carnality of the flesh. The spirit/flesh dichotomy would reach its zenith in certain Christian theologies such as Manicheanism, which taught that salvation was achieved through total rejection of the flesh and its earthly desires.

Related to this concept was the idea of original sin. It refers to the first sin committed by Adam and Eve and extends the consequences of that sin to all their offspring. St. Augustine argued that every human born after Adam and Eve, having been born through the carnal channel of the flesh, was tainted with original sin. He saw the world with its manifest evils and cruelties as evidence of the enduring power of original sin. Humankind could not of its own accord control the sinful or evil impulses within. It was only through God's grace that a person could will to do good, and through Christ's intervention, overcome the temptations of the flesh and hence achieve salvation. Thus St. Augustine irrevocably tied the spirit/flesh dichotomy to the concepts of good and evil.

Appendix B
Edgar Cayce's Life and Work

Edgar Cayce is considered by many to be America's best-known and well-documented psychic. He is also considered to be the "father" of holistic medicine. Throughout his life he gave more than 14,000 psychic readings. Over 9,000 were physical readings that dealt with health issues and physical ailments. Nearly 2,000 were life readings, which dealt with a person's potential and purpose in life. The remaining readings were given on various philosophical and historical topics.

Cayce believed the source of the readings to be two-fold: 1) the subconscious mind of the individual for whom he was giving the reading; and, 2) the Akashic Records, which can be thought of as the "collective unconscious" of humanity, a type of universal database in which every thought, word, or deed that has ever transpired in the earth or beyond it is recorded.

Cayce never claimed to have special abilities nor did he ever consider himself to be exceptional in any way. He maintained that each individual possesses some type of psychic ability, although it manifests in different ways in different people. He never charged for his readings, although he did accept donations in later years. In fact, he and his family led a life of relative poverty, at times barely having enough money to pay the rent. Rather than trying to convert people to the readings' philosophy, they were advised to incorporate the information into their own religious and belief systems.

The readings never offered a set of beliefs that had to be embraced, but instead focused on the fact that each person should test the principles presented in her own life. Although a staunch Christian in his own beliefs, Cayce's work stressed the importance of comparative study among different belief systems. The underlying principle of the readings is the oneness of all life, tolerance for all people, and a compassion and understanding for all religions.

Cayce was born near Hopkinsville, Kentucky, in 1877, and had a normal childhood in most respects, with one exception. He displayed psychic abilities at an early age. At the age of six, he told his parents that he could see and talk to relatives who had recently died. Like most families, they attributed these experiences to an overactive imagination. Raised in a fundamentalist Christian family, he found comfort in reading the Bible and decided to read it through from cover to cover, once for every year of his life. At the age of thirteen, he had an experience that would affect him deeply. A beautiful woman had appeared to him in a vision and asked him what he most wanted in life. He responded that he wanted to help others, especially children. In later life his psychic gifts would allow him to do just that. In order to help out his family financially, Cayce left school as a teenager and started working with an uncle on his grandmother's farm, giving up his dream of becoming a doctor or a minister.

As a young man, Cayce held several jobs, including working in a bookstore and a dry goods store. He later became a traveling insurance salesman. He was stricken with chronic laryngitis, however, and this ended his career as an insurance salesman. He returned to Hopkinsville and eventually found what he thought was the perfect job as a photographer's assistant. He became engaged to Gertrude Evans.

In an effort to cure his laryngitis, Cayce agreed to consult a local hypnotist. During a session with Al Layne, he diagnosed the cause of and cure for his chronic laryngitis condition. When he awakened, Cayce was able to speak normally for the first time in almost a year, although he could not remember what he had said in this "sleep state." Cayce was sure that he could now get married and get on with a normal life. Mr. Layne, however, had other ideas for he believed he had seen something truly extraordinary. He asked Cayce to give another "reading" on his own stomach problems. Although skeptical, Cayce agreed as he felt he owed Layne for having helped him regain his voice. During the reading Cayce diagnosed the problem and recommended herbal medicines, foods, and exercises for improvement. After one week of following these recommendations, Layne improved greatly.

Layne now began to encourage Cayce to explore his unique talent. Cayce was reluctant to do so, however. Layne argued that he had a moral obligation to pursue this work if his talent could help people. Gertrude also pointed out that this gift might be the answer to what he had been seeking for so long—a way to help others. After a great deal of prayer, conversations with his family, and consulting the Bible for guidance, Cayce agreed to continue, with two conditions. The first was that if he ever suggested anything in the sleep state that could be harmful, they would stop the readings. The second was that Layne had to always remember that Edgar Cayce was first, and foremost, a photographer.

In the years that followed, Cayce continued to give "physical readings" for hundreds of people while he worked as a photographer. During the readings, he diagnosed the cause of and recommended treatment for dozens of physical aliments. Although still somewhat uncomfortable with the readings, his life was fulfilling. He had a loving wife, a home, a Sunday school class at the local church, and a good job. A year later he formed his own photographic partnership and was able to open a studio. His Sunday school classes became the most popular in the county because of Cayce's ability to make the Bible come alive. In 1923, he hired Gladys Davis as a secretary to take down the information he gave during the readings while Gertrude asked her "sleeping" husband the questions.

Until 1923, most of Cayce's readings were limited to medical and physical conditions. That year a printer from Dayton, Ohio, who had obtained successful readings for two of his nieces, asked Cayce for a horoscope reading. At the end of the reading (5717-1) Cayce made an unexpected remark by saying, "he was once a monk."

This statement caused Cayce and his family much concern and doubt, and led to a great deal of soul-searching, as this reference to reincarnation was contrary to their fundamental Christian beliefs. During a reading where Cayce asked for guidance, he was advised to read the Bible once through from cover to cover while keeping the idea of reincarnation in mind. The underlying philosophy that emerged was one that focused upon the oneness and the purposefulness of life. In time, Cayce, like many others, realized that reincarnation was not incompatible with Christianity but was actually a long-forgotten tenet of that faith.

After this, Cayce also gave "life readings" that dealt with an individual's previous lifetimes, as well as the person's potential and purpose in the present. In time, the topics in the readings were expanded to include mental and spiritual counsel, philosophy, spirituality, meditation, dream interpretation, intuition, history, and even advice for improving personal relationships.

In September of 1925, the Cayce family moved with Gladys Davis to Virginia Beach. In 1927, friends and backers of Cayce formed the Association of National Investigators for the purpose of further researching and testing the information contained in the readings. The Association's motto was, "That We May Make Manifest Our Love for God and Man." The next year, the Edgar Cayce hospital opened its doors. Patients came from all over the country to obtain readings and to be treated by a qualified staff composed of doctors, nurses, and therapists. In June of 1931, the Association for Research and Enlightenment, Inc. (A.R.E.) was formed as a research body whose goal was to investigate and disseminate the information contained in Cayce's readings.

As his fame as a psychic grew, so did the number of skeptics. Many people came to Virginia Beach to expose him as a fraud. All left convinced of the legitimacy of his work. One staunch Catholic writer, named Thomas Sugrue, came to Virginia Beach to investigate what he thought had to be trickery. He became a close friend to Cayce, and ended up writing *There is a River*, a biography of Cayce published in 1943, and a perennial best seller.

During World War II, sacks of mail were delivered to Cayce with ever-growing requests for readings. Despite the readings' warning that he should give no more than two readings per day, Cayce often gave up to eight per day in an effort to keep up with requests. In the spring of 1944, this began to take a toll on his health. His own readings advised him to rest, but he felt a tremendous obligation to those who were asking for his help. Shortly afterwards, he had a stroke and became partially paralyzed. He told his friends that he would be "healed" after the first of the year; they understood that he meant he would pass into the spirit realm and return home. He died on January 3, 1945. Gertrude died three months later on Easter Sunday.

Gladys Davis continued Cayce's work; she took charge of cataloguing and indexing the readings. Because of the number of readings as well as the follow-up reports and documentation, the project was not finished until 1971, more than a quarter century after Cayce had died. Once indexed, the readings covered an astonishing 10,000 different subjects. Gladys chaired the computerization of the readings until her death in 1986 at the age of eighty-one. Today, the complete set of Cayce readings is available on CD-Rom.

Several organizations work with the information contained in the Edgar Cayce readings. The Association for Research and Enlightenment, Inc. (A.R.E.), headquartered in Virginia Beach, Virginia, continues to make the material readily available to seekers worldwide. It boasts one of the largest libraries on metaphysical subjects in the country. The organization is committed to spiritual growth, holistic healing, psychic research, parapsychology, and metaphysical studies. The Edgar Cayce Foundation is a separate organization that is legally responsible for the readings. It spends time and resources sponsoring comparative studies between the Cayce information and other schools of thought. Atlantic University offers a master's degree in Transpersonal Studies. The Cayce/Reilly Massage School trains therapists from around the world in the therapeutic benefits of massage.

From 1901 to 1944, Edgar Cayce gave over 14,000 readings covering 10,000 subjects. Over 300 books have been written on Cayce's work. The accuracy of his physical readings continues to amaze modern day medical professionals. The consistency within the 14,000 readings, spanning over forty years, attests to their authenticity. This is why the Edgar Cayce readings are considered to be the most accurate and thoroughly documented source of metaphysical information in the world today.

Those seeking additional information on Edgar Cayce and his work are referred to the official A.R.E. website: www.edgarcayce.org.

Appendix C
The Root Races

The First Root Race refers to the first group of souls to enter the earth plane. They did so while still in spirit form and were able to enter and exit matter at will. In their desire to experience as many physical sensations as possible, they inhabited the bodies of animals that already existed on earth. As they spent increasing periods of time in animal bodies, they gradually lost the awareness of their true identity as spiritual beings. They came to believe they were the physical forms in which they were trapped. Most were unable to free themselves from their self-created physical hell until after the death of the physical body. Even then their confusion following this experience remained great and some were unable to find their way back to the light of the Creative Force without help from other spiritual beings.

The First Root Race is likely the source of the half-man/half-beast creatures of myth and legend. Stories of angels who interbred with humans are also a likely reflection of the time when souls first took on physical form in the earth and misapplied their creative powers. As noted in Chapter Four, one such tale is told in the Book of Enoch, which tells the story of Azazel and Semjaza, the Watchers who incited angels to descend to earth and take human women as wives. The offspring of this unnatural union were hideous, monstrous beings that fought amongst themselves and brought great evil to the earth. They were finally destroyed when God intervened and caused the Biblical flood to destroy all life except that which is safe with Noah on his ark.

The Second Root Race refers to the soul group that entered the earth plane in an attempt to help those who had come before and were now trapped in matter. Their motive for incarnating was a sincere desire to help their lost brethren regain a sense of their spiritual being. Many of these souls had already incarnated in physical form on other worlds and thought their task an easy one. They entered the earth plane in the form of a "light body." Although this light body appeared to have a human form, though somewhat taller and more elongated than our present day form, it was more highly compacted energy than matter. These souls also possessed the ability to project themselves into other forms of matter at will.

There was something different about this world, however, and many of these souls fell prey to the same desires as the group that preceded them. They too lost sight of their spiritual nature and became trapped in matter. Those few who resisted the lure of dense physical forms were reluctant to leave the earth plane believing that they had failed in their mission to help their brethren.

Memories of this soul group live on in the stories of the mythical land of Lemuria. Lemurians are also the true source for the legends of shape-shifters that abound in many cultures, particularly among Native American peoples. The Book of Jubilees may also be based on the ancient Lemurians. In this story angels came to earth to teach righteousness, only to find themselves seduced by human women. This myth might very well tell the tale of those souls, still in unity consciousness, who came to earth to help those who had lost their way.

The third group of souls to incarnate in the earth plane entered the physical dimension more as a thought body, rather than dense flesh bodies. "...it is seen that individuals in the beginning were more of thought forms than individual entities with personalities as seen in the present." (364-10) These bodies were less dense than those we presently inhabit. The difference between the Third Root Race and those that preceded it was that this group came with a plan. They were to develop the perfect vehicle—the human body—for the soul to inhabit while in the earth.

The human body would allow the soul to experience the opportunities materiality presented while at the same time allowing it to retain a conscious memory of its true nature as a spiritual being. The creation of this body did not happen overnight, however. It was done in accordance with the natural evolutionary laws of the physical world. The achievements of the Third Root Race are remembered in the tales of the legendary land of Atlantis.

A more thorough explanation of this time in human history is far beyond the scope of this book. Those desiring more information on the soul groups can refer to *Our Origin & Destiny, An Evolutionary Perspective on the New Millennium*, Kathy L. Callahan, Virginia Beach, Virginia: A.R.E. Press, 1996.

ABOUT THE AUTHOR

Author and lecturer, Kathy L. Callahan, Ph.D., is a career Naval officer with the rank of Captain. She has an educational background in Anthropology, with a M.S. and Ph.D. from Purdue University. She wrote her doctoral thesis on alcoholism treatment among the urban Tohono O'Odham (Papago Indians). She has been a student of the Edgar Cayce readings for over 30 years, and has presented workshops at A.R.E. Headquarters and field conferences. She has also been a student of *A Course in Miracles* for 14 years. She teaches courses and workshops on a variety of subjects including the Universal Laws. She is a frequent speaker at Unity Churches and has appeared on radio and television including *Sightings* and *The Unexplained*. Her other books include *Unseen Hands and Unknown Hearts,* which tells the story of her daughter's miraculous healing from a life-threatening illness, *Our Origin and Destiny, an Evolutionary Perspective on the New Millennium*, which discusses the development of the multisensory human, and *Living in the Spirit, Applying Spiritual Truth in Daily Life,* a how-to book on the practice of spiritual truth as a means to create good in your life. She currently resides in Fairfax, Virginia.

ENDNOTES

Author's Foreword
[1] Refer to Beane, Wendell Charles, "Good versus Evil, Enlightenment Beyond Terrorism," *Venture Inward,* January/February 2002, pg. 14-17.

Introduction
[2] The Christian concept of heaven and hell is based upon the law of karma. Those who obey God's commandments and do good in their earthly lives will be rewarded in the afterlife while those who disobey God's laws and commit evil acts are condemned to an existence of pain and suffering in Hell.
[3] Swiss psychologist Carl G. Jung believed that archetypes arise from the "collective unconscious," the part of the human psyche that contains the common psychological inheritance of humanity. They are primordial images that reside in the collective unconscious of the individual. Scholars believe that the study of archetypes—the transcendent reality that underlies physical manifestations—may be the best key to understanding the complexities of human behavior.
[4] The term *metaphysics* originally referred to the writings of Aristotle that came after his writings on physics, as made in the arrangement by Andronicus of Rhodes, three centuries after Aristotle's death.
[5] Refer to Studebaker, Alden, *Wisdom for a Lifetime,* Unity Village, Missouri: Unity Books, 1998.

Chapter One: Good and Evil as Cosmic Forces
[6] Lucas, George, *The Star Wars: From the Adventures of Luke Skywalker,* New York: Ballantine Books, 1986.
[7] Frost, S.E. Jr., *Basic Teachings of the Great Philosophers,* New York: Double Day, 1962, p. 129.

8 While the Stoics referred to nature and Logos as one and the same, Logos actually referred to nature's overall rational structure that provided the ordering principle for all that exists.

9 Guiley, Rosemary Ellen, *Harpers Encyclopedia of Mystical and Paranormal Experience*, San Francisco: Harper, 1991, p. 453.

10 The most celebrated writings of Plato include the *Republic*, the *Symposium*, the *Phaedo*, the *Phaedrus*, and the *Timaeus*, all written in dialogue form. Plato's teacher Socrates left behind no writings of his own. His philosophical ideas are thus presented to us through Plato's interpretation.

11 Plato's use of the word idea came from the Greek *eidos*, which denoted the form, pattern or essential quality of a thing. To Plato, ideas are objective and independent of human thought. This is different from the modern usage of "idea" that refers to a subjective mental construct specific to an individual mind. For that reason I prefer to use the word "Form" to denote Plato's Ideas. Refer to Tarnas, Richard, *The Passion of the Western Mind*, New York: Ballantine Books, 1991, p. 10.

Chapter Two: Good and Evil Personified

12 In Greek mythology, Zeus is the ruler of heaven and earth, and both gods and mortals. As the ruler or "father of the gods" he represents a figure of authority and control who enforces discipline among the other gods. He also watches over humankind and metes out punishment for wrongdoing. As an authority figure it would seem logical that he represent the concept of good. Yet Zeus is very "human" when it comes to his own desires. His frequent amorous alliances with females, divine and mortal, are a source of irritation to his wife Hera, and often result in tragedy for mortals unfortunate enough to become involved in their divine intrigues.

The god Apollo presents similar contrasts in behavior. Apollo is the god of law and wisdom. He was known as a proponent of moderation and adherence to a moral code of behavior. Yet Apollo was also associated with the Oracle at Delphi, where he killed the evil serpent Python and founded the renowned center of prophecy. Many of his followers participated in passionate rituals designed to induce a state of ecstasy whereby they might know the mysteries of life.

13 Manicheanism professed the principle of absolute dualism and a primal conflict between good and evil. It also denied the reality of Christ's body and rejected the idea of free will. Evil was seen as a physical entity and women were considered forces of darkness that bound men to the evils of the flesh. St. Augustine wrote and spoke against it in later life. This sect was later declared a heresy by the Byzantine emperor Justinian.

Chapter Three: Of Angels and Demons
14 Pseudo-Dionysus was a Greek writer who wrote extensively on Christian mysticism and angelology. His major works include *The Celestial Hierarchy, The Mystical Theology and Ecclesiastical Hierarchy,* and *The Divine Names.* It is possible that his writings represent the collaboration of more than one person. They show evidence of a strong Platonic influence and in turn had a profound impact on medieval Christian scholars including St. Thomas Aquinas and St. John of the Cross. They later influenced the works of John Milton and Dante. For further information refer to *Pseudo-Dionysus: The Compete Works,* New York: The Paulist Press, 1987.

15 In Kabbalah, the Tree of Life is the central image of meditation. The Tree shows the descent of the divine into the material world and the path by which the soul can ascend to the divine. The Tree consists of ten *sephirot,* each of which represents an attribute of God, and are

described by a name of God. The seven lower sephirot are Sovereignty, Foundation, Endurance, Majesty, Beauty, Loving-kindness and Judgment. The top three sephirot are Understanding, Wisdom, and Crown (Humility), and represent the mystical steps to union with God. Refer to Berenson-Perkins, Janet, *Kabbalah Decoder*, New York: Barron's Educational Series, 2000.

Chapter Four: Historic Concepts of Satan
[16] As quoted in Tremmel, William C., *Dark Side, The Satan Story*, St. Louis, Missouri: CBP Press, 1987, p. 65.

Chapter Five: Secular Thought
[17] Human nature refers to the intrinsic characteristics, qualities, and disposition of the human species. Taken from *The American Heritage Dictionary of the English Language*, New College Edition, Morris William, editor, Boston: Houghton Mifflin Company, 1976, p. 875.
[18] Refer to Tarnas, previously cited, pg. 328-329.
[19] Refer to Fromm, Eric, *The Anatomy of Human Destructiveness*, New York: Holt, Rinehart and Winston, 1973.
[20] The chest thumping displays observed by humans turned out to be communicative displays which did not result in actual violence or harm to another.
[21] It has been speculated that some of the apparently aggressive behavior demonstrated by the Gombe chimps in later years might have been influenced by the continued presence of human observation and encroachment upon their territory.
[22] Montagu, Ashley, *The Human Revolution*, New York: 1965, p. 8.

Chapter Six: The Universal Forces
[23] Refer to Robertson, Jon, *The Golden Thread of Oneness*, Virginia Beach, Virginia: A.R.E. Press, 1997.

Chapter Seven: The Origin of Evil

[24] *A Course in Miracles*, Tiburon, California: Foundation for Inner Peace, 1985.

[25] Note the similarity between this quotation and "the impossible thought of separation" as presented in *A Course in Miracles*.

[26] For a more detailed explanation of the material dimension, refer to "Spirit," *A Search for God*, Book Two, Virginia Beach, Virginia: A.R.E. Press, 1988.

[27] "Opportunity," *A Search for God*, Book Two, previously cited, 1988, p. 3.

Chapter Eight: The Reality of Evil

[28] Those familiar with Christian theology may notice a similarity between this idea and the doctrine of *privatio boni*, which states that evil has no substance of its own but exists only as a lessening of the good. It was first suggested by Aristotle and later adopted by Origen, St. Augustine, St. Thomas Aquinas, and many others.

[29] See Thurston, Mark, "The Problem of Good and Evil," *More Great Teachings of Edgar Cayce*, Virginia Beach, Virginia: A.R.E. Press, 1997. Refer also to Fox, Matthew, *Sins of the Spirit, Blessings of the Flesh, Lessons for Transforming Evil in Soul and Society*, New York: Three Rivers Press, 1999.

Chapter Nine: The Function of Evil

[30] Taken from Maag, Victor, "The Antichrist," *Evil*, Evanston, Illinois: Northwestern University Press, 1967.

[31] Refer to Sanford, John A., *Evil, The Shadow Side of Reality*, New York: The Crossroad Publishing Company, 1998.

[32] Samuels, et.al., *A Critical Dictionary of Jungian Analysis*, London, 1986.

[33] *The Collective Works of C.G. Jung*. Volume 16, paragraph 470.

[34] Samuels, previously cited, p. 138.
[35] Sanford, previously cited, p. 41.
[36] For further information on the multisensory human, refer to Callahan, Kathy L., *Our Origin and Destiny, An Evolutionary Perspective on the New Millennium*, Virginia Beach, Virginia: A.R.E. Press, 1996.

Chapter Ten: Synthesis
[37] Buber, Martin, *Good and Evil*, New Jersey: Prentice-Hall, Inc., 1953, p. 66.
[38] Fromm, previously cited, p. 432.
[39] Zukav, Gary, *The Seat of the Soul*, New York: Simon & Schuster, Inc., 1989, p. 70.
[40] See also Cayce, Edgar Evans, *Edgar Cayce on Atlantis*, New York: Warner Books, 1968.
[41] According to the Catholic Encyclopedia, Belial is a personal name in the Vulgate and various English translations of the Bible, commonly used as a synonym of Satan (II Corinthians v. 15). In the Vulgate translation of III Kings 23:10-13, the same Hebrew word is rendered once as Belial and twice as the devil. Other meanings include "vile scoundrels" (Judges 14:22), and "destruction" (Psalm 12:9). Its use in the readings is likely as an analogy for those who seek to follow the influence of evil. Cayce never indicated this name referred to an actual god or being.
[42] Fox, previously cited, p. 155.

Appendix A: Archetypes of Good and Evil
[43] Fox, previously cited, p. 11.
[44] Zukav, previously cited, p. 70.

ISBN 141201751-3

9 781412 017510

Printed in Great Britain
by Amazon